THE SEEKER'S JOURNEY

FROM SCIENCE TO SELF

Deepak Sekar

Made with ❤ on the Notion Press Platform

www.notionpress.com

DEDICATION

To the Seeker,
who has wandered through stars and scriptures,
through silence and suffering,
only to arrive at the door of their own heart.

To the Light within me,
which has never ceased to whisper —
even when I forgot to listen.

To the ancient ones —
the Siddhars, Rishis, Yogis, and mystics —
whose breath still echoes in every sacred word of this book.

To my past self,
who was brave enough to break,
and to my future self,
who will remember why.

And to the Eternal,
the One without name,
who dances through every moment —
seen and unseen —
and called this book into being.

TABLE OF CONTENTS

PREFACE

This book begins with a simple, yet profound intention: to remember where it all began.

In these pages, I trace the journey that has led me to this very moment — reflecting on the choices I've made, the pivotal moments that shaped me, and the quiet inner shifts that have transformed the very essence of who I am. This is not just a record of events, but a personal exploration, a search for deeper understanding that spans years of self-inquiry.

As I write this, my aim is to document my evolution — so that, years from now, I can look back and reconnect with the version of myself who once stood at the edge of discovery, questioning, wondering, seeking. I want to remember how far I've come, the lessons learned, and the wisdom gained along the way.

This book is deeply personal. It is written by me, for me, and ultimately about me. But more than that, it is an invitation — an invitation to anyone who has ever stood at the crossroads of their own journey, asking the same questions, wondering about the same mysteries. It is a reflection of my path, yes, but also a mirror to yours. It is both a record of my story and a map of the deeper truths we all share, waiting to be uncovered.

INTRODUCTION

At some point in our lives, most of us ask big questions: What is life? Why am I here? What is the meaning of all this?

These are not new questions. People have been asking them for thousands of years. Some look to science for answers. Others turn to religion or spirituality. And sometimes, we find ourselves standing between the two—science on one side, spirituality on the other—wondering if they can both be true.

This book is born from that wonder. It's a journey across both worlds—science and spirit—to see if they're really so different after all. Through this journey, I've come to believe that science and spirituality are not enemies. In fact, they can work together to help us understand the universe, and ourselves, more deeply.

My Own Search

I started my search with science. I loved how it explained the world— how planets move, how atoms behave, how life evolves. Science gave me tools to explore, discover, and understand.

But then came the questions that science couldn't answer. Questions about meaning, consciousness, and why anything exists at all. Science could describe how things work, but not why they matter. That's when I realized I needed to look somewhere else too.

That somewhere else was spirituality—not religion in the traditional sense, but a personal exploration of what lies beyond what we can see and measure.

An Invitation to You

You don't need to be a scientist or a monk to take this journey. All you need is curiosity. An open heart. A willingness to ask deep questions—even when there are no easy answers.

This book isn't here to preach or prove. It's here to explore. To connect the dots between the physical and the spiritual. Between the seen and the unseen. Between you and the universe.

So let's begin—with wonder, with sincerity, and with a quiet hope that somewhere in the middle of science and spirit, we'll find something true.

PART I
THE HUMAN QUEST
FOR TRUTH

CHAPTER 1
WHERE IT ALL BEGAN

It all started in school, where I first fell in love with science.

Among all the subjects, it was physics that truly captivated me. There was something about the way it revealed the hidden laws behind everyday phenomena — how the universe functioned, how time and space interacted, how forces invisible to the eye governed everything around us. Science didn't just teach facts; it gave me a new way of seeing.

I wasn't just learning; I was awakening.

Each discovery felt like unlocking a deeper layer of reality. I would read, observe, and question relentlessly, driven by a hunger to understand not just the how, but the very essence of the world I lived in.

As I approached the end of my school years, I had to make a decision about my future. Choosing engineering felt like a natural extension of my love for science — a way to apply that curiosity and transform knowledge into tangible outcomes. I embraced it fully, not out of obligation, but with genuine passion. Everything I studied seemed to add another brushstroke to the ever-expanding canvas of understanding.

The world became a web of interconnected systems, and I loved seeing through that lens. It felt like I was exactly where I was meant to be.

But life had more to teach — in ways I hadn't expected.

Alongside my academic journey, a parallel experience began to unfold — one that had nothing to do with textbooks or theories. It was about emotions, human connections, vulnerability, and the unpredictable terrain of love.

I met someone.

Through them, I learned about joy, trust, companionship — but also about pain, confusion, and heartbreak. I had once believed that science explained everything, but this was different. Emotions couldn't be calculated. Relationships couldn't be solved like equations.

At one point, I truly believed that this person gave my life meaning — that they were the answer I had been looking for.

But then, without warning, it all fell apart.

Everything I thought was stable, everything I believed to be true, disappeared. The connection we had, the presence I once felt, simply vanished. I was left with silence where there had once been certainty. What I had built my emotional world upon had crumbled, and I didn't know what to hold onto anymore.

In the aftermath of that loss, something changed in me.

I began to ask questions I had never asked before — not just about life, but about existence itself.

"What is life really about?"
"Why are we born?"
"What's the point of going through joy and suffering, connection and loss?"
"Is there a purpose behind it all — or is it just chaos dressed up in meaning?"

Naturally, I turned back to science — my old refuge. But this time, I found it lacking. Science could describe the mechanics of the universe with

breathtaking precision. It could explain the how behind almost anything —
the Big Bang, evolution, consciousness, gravity. But it couldn't answer the
why.

Why did the Big Bang happen in the first place? Why is there
something rather than nothing? Why do we feel the things we do, and what
are we meant to do with those feelings? These weren't questions that
formulas or theories could resolve.

I had never believed in God. Like many others who are drawn to
science, I had dismissed the idea because it couldn't be empirically proven.
Faith had always seemed like a crutch for those unwilling to face the
unknown.

But as I stood in the vast emptiness left by my unanswered questions, I
began to wonder if maybe, just maybe, the answers I was looking for lay
beyond the realm of science. Not instead of it — but beyond it.

And so, this book was born. It is my attempt to make sense of the
questions that science can't answer — to explore life, existence, and
meaning from every angle available to me.

I don't know if I'll find all the answers.
Maybe I'll never find them at all.
But I am committed to the search.
That, in itself, feels like a kind of purpose.

Let's begin.

CHAPTER 2
WHAT IS SCIENCE, REALLY?

To most, it begins as a subject in school — formulas to memorize, diagrams to label, facts to repeat. But for me, science has always been something more than ink on a page or experiments in a lab. It is a way of seeing. A method of peeling back the surface of the world to reveal what lies underneath. At its heart, science is humanity's most sincere attempt to understand the universe — not as we hope it to be, but as it truly is.

Science begins with a question: Why? How? And it never stops asking.

It demands evidence, not assumptions. Clarity, not comfort. In that way, it's both humbling and empowering — a tool that helps us explore the vastness of space, the intricacies of nature, the very fabric of reality itself. It teaches us that we are not at the center of the universe, but we are capable of understanding it. And for me, that's where the wonder begins.

Among all the sciences, physics has always felt the most fundamental — the closest to the root of existence. It doesn't just describe the things in the universe; it explains the laws that govern them. Why an apple falls to the ground. Why planets orbit stars. Why electricity flows, and light bends, and time stretches. Physics is the architecture of reality — the invisible blueprint written into the bones of the cosmos.

For centuries, our understanding of the physical world was shaped by classical physics — the mechanics of motion, force, gravity, and energy. It was neat, elegant, and astonishingly predictive. You could calculate precisely how far a ball would travel, how long it would take a planet to orbit the sun, or how much energy it would take to launch a rocket. The universe, it seemed, was a vast and orderly machine — predictable, logical, almost mechanical.

And then, the ground shifted beneath our feet.

Quantum physics emerged — and with it, a new reality that defied everything we thought we knew.

In the subatomic world, the rules are different. Particles behave like waves. Matter can exist in multiple states at once. An electron doesn't have a single location — it has a probability of being in many places, until we observe it. And in that moment of observation, it 'chooses' a state. As if reality itself waits for us to look before it decides how to behave.

Even more bizarre: two particles can become linked — "entangled" — so that changing one instantly affects the other, no matter how far apart they are. It's as though the universe has a hidden thread connecting everything in ways we're only beginning to comprehend.

This isn't just strange — it's revolutionary. The world beneath the surface isn't just uncertain. It's deeply mysterious. Unpredictable. Perhaps even unknowable.

And that brings me to a question that won't leave me alone:

If the foundations of the universe are built on probabilities, uncertainties, and unseen connections… what does that say about us?

We, too, are made of atoms. The same particles. The same quantum rules. So where does that leave free will? Consciousness? Identity? Are we merely collections of particles following physical laws — elaborate machines made of stardust and chance? Or is there something more — something that transcends the mathematics?

Why are we here?
What is the purpose of life?
Is there a reason behind existence, or are we drifting through a cosmic accident, assigning meaning as we go?

These are not questions science has clear answers for. And yet, they are the very questions that led me to science in the first place.

This journal is my way of chasing those questions — not with dogma or blind belief, but with open eyes and a curious mind. I don't expect definitive answers. Science doesn't always provide them. What it offers instead is a commitment to truth, however uncomfortable or uncertain that truth may be.

It tells us that we may never understand everything — but we are allowed to ask.

We are invited to explore. And perhaps, in the search itself, we begin to uncover not just how the universe works — but who we are within it.

CHAPTER 3
THE BEAUTY OF UNCERTAINTY

One of the most fascinating — and, admittedly, strangest — aspects of quantum physics is something known as *uncertainty*. At the tiniest scales of reality, inside atoms and subatomic particles, the world doesn't follow the neat, predictable rules we're used to. Instead, it becomes fuzzy, fluid, and full of mystery.

At that scale, you can't know both the exact position of a particle and how fast it's moving at the same time. The more precisely you measure one, the less certain you become about the other. This isn't a flaw in our instruments — it's a fundamental limit built into the nature of reality itself. This principle, discovered by Werner Heisenberg, is fittingly called the Heisenberg Uncertainty Principle.

That might sound deeply technical, but here's a simple way to imagine it:

Picture yourself in a dark room with a fly buzzing around. You quickly flash a light and glimpse the fly near the wall. But the very act of shining that light — of observing it — causes it to move. By the time you walk over, it's gone. Your attempt to see it changed its behavior. That's what happens in the quantum world: the act of observation alters what is being observed.

And it gets even stranger.

In quantum physics, particles don't seem to settle on a single position or state until we measure them. Until that moment, they exist in a state of superposition — a blend of all the possibilities at once. It's not that we just don't know where they are. It's that they literally haven't chosen to be anywhere specific until they're observed.

In other words, the universe doesn't commit to a reality until something — or someone — is watching.

So why does any of this matter to us?

After all, we live in a world of cars, coffee, conversations — not subatomic particles. Our lives seem far too large and stable to behave like quantum systems.

And yet, we are made of particles. The same fundamental building blocks. And while quantum effects might not directly govern our day-to-day experiences, they might still echo in the fabric of our thoughts, decisions, and sense of identity. Some scientists and philosophers have even speculated that quantum uncertainty could play a subtle role in consciousness, creativity, and free will.

A Glimpse Into Life Through Uncertainty

Here's a simple way to think about how quantum uncertainty reflects life itself:

Imagine you're planning your future. You weigh job offers, think about relationships, consider where you want to live. You do your best to analyze everything logically — salary, benefits, stability. You're trying to measure the "momentum" of your life — where you're heading, and how fast.

But at the same time, other parts of life — like how this decision will affect your happiness, your relationships, or your mental peace — are harder to predict. That's like trying to measure your "position" in life. The more you fixate on one variable, the blurrier the other becomes.

This is where quantum uncertainty becomes more than a scientific curiosity — it becomes a metaphor.

The more we try to lock down every aspect of life, the more we realize that some things remain unknowable. You might pour energy into shaping your career, only to discover later that your personal life has shifted in ways you didn't expect. Or you might chase clarity in love, and find your goals drifting. Life is a moving target — a constantly shifting interplay of variables.

Trying to control everything is not only impossible — it's exhausting.

Just like in quantum mechanics, we can't pin everything down. We can't predict every outcome. And maybe we're not meant to. Maybe life, like the quantum world, thrives on uncertainty.

Superposition of the Mind

Think about a small moment — deciding whether to text someone or stay silent.

You sit there, hesitating. Part of you wants to reach out. Another part of you isn't sure. You're in a kind of emotional superposition — suspended between multiple outcomes, multiple selves. Then, with a flicker of will, you make a choice. You send the message. Or you don't.

In that moment, one version of reality collapses into being. The others fade.

Of course, human choices are shaped by far more than just quantum particles. Emotions, memory, intuition, and biology all play their part. But it's fascinating to consider that even the universe itself doesn't run strictly on cause-and-effect. At its core, it runs on possibilities. On things that aren't fixed until they're acted upon.

To me, that changes how I think about life. Maybe we're not as bound by rigid rules as we assume. Maybe we're not trapped in a single, predetermined path. Maybe — just like the particles that form us — we are part of a universe built on potential. A universe that holds space for change, choice, and discovery.

Uncertainty, then, isn't something to fear. It's something to embrace.

It reminds us that we don't have to have everything figured out. That it's okay not to know all the answers. That growth often comes not from certainty, but from being open to what we cannot yet predict.

After all, some of the most meaningful things in life — love, purpose, transformation — emerge not from control, but from mystery. And maybe, just maybe, the unknown is where the real magic lives. .

CHAPTER 4
ENTANGLEMENT, OBSERVATION, AND THE MYSTERY OF CONNECTION

Now we step into what may be the most beautiful, bewildering, and profoundly unexplainable frontier in all of physics: quantum entanglement, the observer effect, and the haunting possibility that these strange ideas might echo within human consciousness — and even the invisible threads that bind us to one another.

Just when quantum uncertainty begins to stretch our imagination, quantum entanglement arrives and completely unravels the way we think about space, time, and separateness.

Quantum Entanglement: The Universe's Invisible Thread

Quantum entanglement occurs when two particles interact in such a way that their states become inseparably linked. From that moment on, no matter how far apart they drift — across a room, a planet, or even light-years — they remain mysteriously connected. Measure one, and the other instantly reflects the change.

This is not theory; it's been demonstrated repeatedly in laboratories. Even Einstein, skeptical and unsettled by the implications, famously called it **"spooky action at a distance."** He wasn't wrong to be spooked. How could something here affect something there, with no signal traveling between them?

This phenomenon defies our classical understanding of the universe — where things are separate, effects follow causes, and distance means delay.

But entanglement tells a different story: that on some fundamental level, the universe is not made of isolated parts, but of deep, indivisible relationships.

And if the tiniest components of matter can remain connected across vast distances, we are left with a breathtaking question:

Could we be connected, too?

The Echo of Entanglement in Human Experience

We are not exempt from the quantum world — we are composed of it. Every atom in our bodies, every neuron in our brains, dances to the rules of quantum mechanics. So what if this strange interconnectedness doesn't stop at particles? What if it somehow echoes into our thoughts, our emotions, our relationships?

Have you ever thought of someone, only to have them call you? Felt a loved one's joy or pain without a word spoken? Sensed that some invisible link exists between you and another — something that logic cannot explain?

Science has not yet proven that consciousness is a quantum phenomenon. And yet, the existence of entanglement invites us to wonder: *What if connection isn't just emotional or psychological? What if, in some way, it's physical? What if it's real — just beneath the surface of what we can measure?*

Maybe love, empathy, and intuition are not just human inventions, but reflections of a deeper truth written into the structure of reality itself.

The Observer Effect: When Reality Waits to Be Seen

And then, just as our understanding starts to find footing, quantum mechanics pulls the ground from beneath us again — with the observer effect.

In the now-famous double-slit experiment, electrons fired through two slits create a wave-like interference pattern — suggesting they travel through both slits at once, as if they exist in multiple states simultaneously. But here's the twist: the moment we observe them — the instant we place a detector to see which slit they pass through — the wave pattern vanishes. The electrons choose a path. They act like particles, not waves.

Observation collapses possibility into a single outcome.

It's as if the universe is not fixed, but waiting — undefined until something conscious looks in its direction.

That raises a question both poetic and profound:

What does it mean to be an observer in a universe that responds to being observed?

This does not mean we create reality with our minds — at least not in the mystical sense. But it does suggest that consciousness is not separate from the fabric of existence. It may not be a passive witness, but an active participant in how reality unfolds.

Consciousness and the Quantum Mirror

What if consciousness isn't merely a side-effect of neurons firing?
What if awareness — the act of noticing, feeling, perceiving — is as elemental to the universe as space and time?

Some physicists and philosophers have dared to propose exactly that. They suggest that consciousness may not emerge within the universe, but rather that it is a fundamental part of it — woven into its very design, as intrinsic as gravity or light.

If that's true, then being human is not an accident of biology. It's a form of participation. A way the universe becomes aware of itself.

In this light, the observer effect is not just a technicality in a lab experiment. It becomes a metaphor for life: we shape the world around us by how we choose to see it, where we place our attention, and how deeply we engage with what is in front of us.

A Universe That Feels More Alive

Entanglement and observation challenge the idea that the universe is a cold, mechanical place ticking away in isolation. They suggest instead that reality is rich with relationship, responsiveness, and mystery.

They whisper that perhaps nothing — and no one — is ever truly alone. That the boundaries we see between things may be thinner than we imagine. That connection is not just a feeling, but a principle. That awareness is not a bystander, but a participant.

And maybe, just maybe, the universe is not only watching us, but watching with us.

CHAPTER 5
THE MYSTERY OF LIFE AND THE UNIVERSE

After encountering the elegant strangeness of quantum uncertainty, the mind-bending reality of entanglement, and the mysterious role that observation seems to play in shaping outcomes, one cannot help but pause. A deeper, more ancient question begins to stir beneath the surface of scientific facts:

What is life? Why are we here? What does all of this truly mean—for us, for consciousness, for existence itself?

Modern science, at its most fundamental level, tells us that life is the result of an extraordinary arrangement of atoms and molecules. From hydrogen born in the hearts of stars to carbon forged in stellar explosions, we are composed of the very elements scattered across the cosmos. Time, gravity, energy, and the slow alchemy of evolution bring these elements together in increasingly complex forms. And then, somehow, from this raw, indifferent material, something miraculous occurs:

The atoms begin to move with intention. They self-organize. They breathe. They reproduce. They become aware.

But the moment we try to reduce life to chemistry alone, something essential slips through our fingers. Because life is not just a process—it is an experience. It is the ache of longing, the thrill of discovery, the weight of memory, the joy of love. It is the silent, internal knowing that we are. And no equation—no matter how advanced—has yet managed to capture the fullness of that feeling.

So we must ask: **where does that spark come from?**

Is consciousness merely an accident—a rare and fortunate glitch in the machinery of matter? Or is there something more beneath the surface, something unseen, something intrinsic to the very structure of reality itself?

Science doesn't claim to have all the answers. But what it does offer is a powerful lens: one that helps us observe life honestly, humbly, and with a deepening sense of wonder. It teaches us that life is not separate from the universe. It is the universe—arranged in such a way that it can look back upon itself and ask: *Who am I?*

A Quantum Glimpse at Mystery

Let us return for a moment to quantum physics. The world at the smallest scale does not behave in the predictable, linear way that we once assumed. Instead, it whispers a different truth:

- At the subatomic level, particles do not exist in definite states until observed.
- Entangled particles influence each other instantly, across vast distances.
- Observation itself—the act of looking—has the power to shift the outcome of events.

This is not just technical curiosity. It hints at a reality far more fluid, participatory, and mysterious than our senses alone can perceive.

And so we begin to wonder: **If the smallest units of reality behave in such paradoxical and poetic ways, then perhaps life—consciousness, emotion, creativity—is not just a byproduct of matter. Perhaps it is a natural flowering of the universe's deepest potential.**

Why Are We Born?

It is one of the most intimate and universal questions a human being can ask: Why was I born?

There is no single answer, no final chapter that ties every thread. But perhaps the question itself is the beginning of meaning. Maybe we are born simply because the universe, in its infinite play, allows for it—because out of all the chaos, out of all the randomness, something as fragile and luminous as awareness can take shape.

And once we are here, alive, awake, and asking these questions, the mystery deepens. What will we do with this awareness?

We may never uncover a cosmic instruction manual or a written-in-the-stars purpose. But perhaps that is not the point. Maybe we matter not because the universe owes us meaning, but because we are capable of creating it.

Just as two particles entangled across space can shift the behavior of one another, so too can our smallest actions ripple outward with unseen significance. Just as the act of observation alters the course of a quantum event, so too can our conscious presence reshape the world around us.

A Living Mystery

So what is life?

It is a mystery that breathes. A question that walks. A phenomenon that not only exists but knows that it exists.

We are not separate from the universe. We are the universe—curious, conscious, and capable of love.

To live, then, is to honor that miracle. To ask, not just "Why am I here?" but "Now that I am here, how will I live?"

That, perhaps, is the most profound response to the mystery of life: not an answer, but a choice.

CHAPTER 6
CROSSING THE THRESHOLD: FROM KNOWING TO UNDERSTANDING

We began this journey with the most ancient of human questions—those whispers that echo across generations, civilizations, and philosophies:

What is life? Why are we born? What is the purpose of all this?

These are not questions born of idle curiosity. They arise from the core of our being, especially when life becomes quiet enough for us to truly listen. Like many with a rational, inquisitive mind, I turned to the realm that has shaped our modern world the most: science.

I explored the foundational building blocks of reality—atoms, molecules, forces. I ventured into the elegance of Newtonian mechanics, where everything seemed to follow order, law, and reason. But the further I went, the more things began to unravel.

Quantum physics changed everything.

Suddenly, certainty gave way to uncertainty. The observer began to influence the observed. Particles were no longer in one place at one time, but suspended in a cloud of probabilities—until awareness collapsed them into form. Entangled particles communicated across space instantly, defying all classical logic. And through it all, a subtle theme emerged again and again: **consciousness was not outside the equation—it was entangled in it.**

And so, I arrived at a place I never expected to reach. A wall. A threshold. A boundary of the known.

Science had taken me far—astonishingly far. It gave me a glimpse into the architecture of reality, the elegance of natural laws, the miraculous dance of energy and matter. But it could only go so far. It could explain how things worked, but not why they mattered.

It could illuminate the patterns of the cosmos, but not the meaning of being alive within it.

That's when I realized the nature of my quest had changed.

I wasn't looking for more data. I wasn't searching for more equations or newer theories. I was searching for something else entirely: understanding.

And with that realization, I found myself standing at a crossroads.

One path—the scientific one—was deeply familiar, rigorously tested, and beautifully logical. But it stopped just short of the answers I was truly seeking. The other path was unfamiliar. Mysterious. Intangible. And, to be honest, a little uncomfortable.

The path of spirituality.

Not religion. Not dogma. Not blind belief. But a genuine, heartfelt exploration into the depths of awareness, being, and purpose.

For someone who has lived a life anchored in logic and reason, stepping onto this path feels like setting foot on foreign ground. I don't claim to believe in God—not in the way many describe. I don't yet know what I will find here. But what I do know is this:

If I want to continue seeking truth—honestly, courageously, fully—this is the only way forward.

Because beyond the language of science lies another kind of knowing. Not intellectual, but experiential. Not measured, but lived.

So this is where I stand now—at the threshold between two worlds. I'm not abandoning the rational; I'm simply widening the lens. I'm not trading facts for faith, but rather allowing room for that which facts alone cannot hold.

This is my first step into the unknown.
Not with certainty, but with sincerity.
Not with answers, but with a willingness to listen.
Not with belief, but with presence.

Let the journey continue.

CHAPTER 7
A TURNING POINT IN THE SEARCH FOR MEANING

As I continue exploring the fundamental questions that have followed humanity through millennia—**Why are we born? What is our purpose? What is this thing we call life?**—my path has carried me deep into the architecture of science. From the laws of classical physics to the riddles of quantum uncertainty, from particles in motion to the emergence of consciousness, science guided me as far as it could. And what it offered was powerful.

It gave me equations, models, and mechanisms. It explained the how of life in exquisite detail. But when it came to the *why*—the meaning behind the motion, the soul behind the structure—it fell silent.

And so, I now find myself standing at a quiet but profound turning point.

Not out of disillusionment, but out of honesty, I recognize that my quest for truth is no longer purely intellectual. I'm drawn toward a new terrain—one I've observed from a distance, perhaps even resisted. A terrain not ruled by formulas or proofs, but by presence and perception.

Spirituality.

But what is *spirituality*, really?

What Is Spirituality?

At its essence, spirituality is the search for meaning and connection that transcends the physical. It's not confined to rituals, religion, or belief systems—it's more personal, more primal. It is the human desire to touch something beyond ourselves, to ask: **Who am I? Why am I here? What is the true nature of reality?**

Spirituality is the space where mystery is not a problem to be solved but a depth to be experienced. It invites us to step beyond what we know into what we can feel—that quiet knowing that sometimes surfaces in moments of stillness, awe, or heartbreak.

It isn't something you inherit.
It's something you awaken to.

It might come through meditation, a walk in nature, a profound dream, a deep loss, or a moment of inexplicable peace. It is not about escaping the world, but about seeing it with deeper eyes.

Where Did It Begin?

Spirituality has always been with us.

Long before organized religions took form, human beings looked up at the stars and felt wonder. They sat beside rivers and sensed a presence in the flowing water. They watched birth and death and asked, **What lies beyond this?**

Over time, these intuitive experiences evolved into traditions:

- In **Hinduism**, the journey centers on self-realization and freedom from the cycle of rebirth *(moksha)*.
- In **Buddhism**, it's the path of mindfulness and compassion to end suffering.
- In **Sufism**, it's the love-drunk surrender of the ego into the ocean of the Divine.
- The **Stoic philosophers** of ancient Greece taught that peace comes from aligning oneself with the rational flow of the cosmos.

And while their languages, metaphors, and rituals differ, the essence remains unchanged: **There is more to life than what can be seen, touched, or measured.**

The Layers of Spirituality

Spirituality is not a single belief or a one-time revelation. It is a layered unfolding, a path that moves inward, and then outward, in a spiral of discovery:

- **Self-awareness** – Who am I beyond my mind, body, and story?
- **Connection** – How am I linked to all life, to the earth, to the stars?
- **Transcendence** – Can I experience moments beyond thought, beyond ego?
- **Transformation** – How can I evolve into who I truly am meant to be?
- **Compassionate Action** – How do I live from truth while serving the whole?

These layers are not linear steps, but living processes—interwoven, dynamic, and deeply human.

Why This Matters to Me

For someone who has long placed faith in logic, stepping into the realm of spirituality is not without hesitation. It asks me to soften—not to abandon intellect, but to hold it alongside intuition.

Science gave me astonishing tools. But it could not tell me what to do with consciousness—only that I had it. It could not answer the ache I felt when the stars looked too beautiful for randomness. Or why the simplest acts of kindness moved me more than any theorem.

Spirituality may not offer proof, but it offers presence.
It may not be certain, but it is sincere.

And so I begin—not with blind faith, but with open eyes and a willing heart.

I do not know where this road will lead. But I know it leads further— into the depths of being, into the silence between thoughts, into the mystery that has called me since the beginning.

This is my first step.

Into meaning.

Into awareness.

Into the vast unknown.

Let the journey unfold.

PART II
SPIRITUAL ORIGINS AND YOGIC HERITAGE

CHAPTER 8
WHO ARE THE YOGIS AND WHERE DID YOGA BEGIN?

As I began my journey into the profound depths of yogic philosophy, one question continuously resurfaced: **Who were the yogis, and what did they uncover that still speaks to us across thousands of years?**

A yogi is more than someone who practices or follows a set of rituals—a yogi is a seeker. They dedicate themselves to the pursuit of the highest truth, a truth that transcends mere knowledge of the external world. The yogi is driven by a deep, inner quest to understand the self, the universe, and the intricate connection between them. They do not merely accept teachings; they experience them firsthand.

As I ventured deeper, I was led to a fascinating realization: **Where did this extraordinary journey begin?**

Shiva – The First Yogi (Adi Yogi)

In yogic lore, the first yogi is known as Adi Yogi, which translates to "The Original Yogi." This figure is none other than Shiva, a being whose significance extends beyond that of a mythological god. Shiva represents the very wellspring of all yogic wisdom.

According to ancient Indian traditions, over 15,000 years ago, Shiva emerged in the isolated, mystical Himalayas, absorbed in a profound state of stillness. This was not merely a physical stillness; it was a total union with the cosmos, an absolute meditation where he existed as one with the universe. Observers, awestruck yet bewildered, watched him silently, unable to grasp what he was experiencing.

As time passed, seven seekers, undeterred by the mystery, remained by his side, learning in silence. After years of witnessing this silent transmission of wisdom, Shiva turned to them and began teaching. These seven sages became the *Saptarishis (Seven Sages)*, and they carried the knowledge of yoga across the globe.

Whether you see this as mythology or metaphor, one message is clear: *Yoga is not a belief system, but a technology for inner transformation—first realized through direct, personal experience.*

Shiva: Beyond the God, the First Scientist of the Inner World

For much of my life, I viewed Shiva as a figure of worship—a god, a deity to revere, or a symbol captured in stories and stone. But as I delved deeper into the philosophy of yoga, my perception of him began to shift dramatically.

In yogic philosophy, Shiva is not merely a god; he is the first explorer of consciousness.

Shiva is called Adi Yogi—the "First Yogi," the one who unlocked the mysteries of existence not through external experiments or scholarly texts, but through profound inner exploration, meditation, and silence. Shiva did not claim these truths because they were handed to him; he experienced them directly. He lived these truths. He became them.

Shiva wasn't trying to prove anything to anyone. He simply sat in stillness, observing his own being, and realized something remarkable: that the self and the universe are not separate entities, but part of a unified whole.

This insight resonates deeply, especially for someone like me, rooted in the scientific method. Science is the study of the external world—the objective reality. But yoga, and Shiva's teachings, are the exploration of the inner world—the consciousness that perceives and interacts with that external reality.

Maybe Shiva wasn't just a mythological figure created by ancient minds. Maybe he was a being who understood the nature of life, energy, and consciousness long before we coined terms like "quantum physics" or "neuroscience."

Shiva embodies a living possibility for all of us—a reminder of what we too can become, not as a belief, but as a realization. For those of us walking the spiritual path with a scientific mindset, Shiva is less about blind faith and more about direct experience. He represents the first being to have truly understood the essence of existence—not through knowledge handed down by others, but through personal awakening.

"What Has Nothing At All, That Is Shiva"

In the teachings of yoga, Shiva is described as formless. He is the one who has nothing—and this nothingness is the very foundation of everything.

"What has nothing at all, that is Shiva. It is because it has no form or limits, that it is the boundary-less one. If it had something, even a single thing, it would exist with boundaries. But because it has nothing, we call it Shiva."

This nothingness isn't emptiness in the conventional sense; it is the space of infinite potential. It is the essence from which creation arises.

Shiva's realization was that from nothingness, sound was born. And from sound came vibration. And from vibration, creation itself emerged. Sound and creation are inseparably connected. When we align with these vibrations—when we harmonize them—we begin to glimpse the profound interconnection of all existence.

For Shiva, creation wasn't a random act; it was the unfolding of a cosmic symphony, where each vibration, each sound, carried the essence of life itself.

Shiva: A State of Consciousness

Shiva is not simply a name or a figure in mythology; Shiva is a state of consciousness—formless, eternal, and infinite. This is not just a mystical concept, but a state that can be realized through deep introspection and silence, beyond the noise of the self.

For me, as someone whose roots are deeply planted in the logical and rational, this idea is profoundly liberating. Shiva teaches us that the path to self-realization is not a mere intellectual pursuit. It is the recognition that the answers we seek about life, energy, and consciousness already lie within us—waiting to be uncovered.

In the context of modern science, Shiva's teachings offer a bridge between the inner world of consciousness and the outer world of observable phenomena. His realizations predate scientific discovery and offer a blueprint for understanding the very nature of existence.

Shiva is not a god to be worshipped for the sake of blind belief. Instead, he represents a living example of what we can become: beings who have deeply experienced the truth, who understand the interconnectedness of all things. For me, as someone seeking the deeper truths of life, Shiva is a symbol of the potential for direct, personal realization.

Did Each Saptarishi Learn Different Things from Shiva?

The answer is both yes and no.

Yes, because Shiva, known as Adi Yogi, imparted a vast ocean of knowledge. This knowledge spanned from the mastery of meditation, energy, and yogic sciences, to profound insights into the cosmos, body, sound, and creation itself.

But, No, because despite the breadth of this wisdom, the Saptarishis were all taught the complete essence of yoga. Each of them received the full path to liberation—moksha. Yet, based on their unique nature, personal strengths, and the missions they were destined to fulfill, they specialized in different aspects of this grand knowledge.

In short: All were taught the complete way to liberation. Yet, each one carried a distinct strength that they would later use to illuminate the world in their own way.

What Each Saptarishi Learned and Carried Forward

As per ancient traditions and texts, each of the seven Saptarishis specialized in a specific aspect of this immense wisdom. Here's a brief look at what they learned and passed down through the ages:

Rishi Name	Specialization (*Essence*)
Atri	Mastery of mental discipline, concentration, and cosmic balance. *(Mental energy)*
Bhrigu	Profound understanding of karma—flow of time-energy, astrology, and the cyclical nature of life.

Pulastya	Secrets of creation and manifestation—how the universe and beings come into form.
Pulaha	Communion with nature—mastery over the five elements (*earth, water, fire, air, space*).
Kratu	Mastery of the physical body—strengthening the body and prana (*life energy*) for higher practices.
Vasishta	Highest spiritual wisdom—guiding society and kings, establishing dharma (*right living*).
Angirasa	Sound energy (*mantras*)—using vibration and sound to elevate consciousness.

A Simple Example:

Imagine Shiva, in his infinite wisdom, gifted a treasure chest brimming with spiritual treasures:

- Meditation
- Yoga
- Mantras
- Energy mastery
- Karma knowledge
- Physical techniques
- Mastery over nature

Each of the Saptarishis, guided by their own inner calling, selected the gifts that most resonated with their nature. And then, each one carried their treasure to different corners of the world, planting seeds of wisdom that would later grow into various spiritual paths and practices.

The wisdom of the Saptarishis is recorded in some of the oldest and most revered texts of India:

- Rig Veda
- Mahabharata
- Puranas (such as Vishnu Purana, Shiva Purana)
- Tamil Siddha Texts (like Tirumandiram)

However, over thousands of years, much of the profound knowledge became fragmented and symbolic. The teachings became more poetic, and in some cases, elusive to the modern mind. Yet, the Siddha tradition in Tamil Nadu preserved much of the deeper yogic sciences, keeping the teachings that connect directly to Shiva and the Saptarishis.

This is not merely a "story" woven for entertainment—it's a memory embedded in the very fabric of energy, culture, and tradition.

The truth of this knowledge is not only preserved in sacred texts but can also be found in:

- **Ancient temple carvings,**
- **Yoga and meditation systems,**
- **Siddha medicine and healing sciences,**
- **Cultural parallels** seen across ancient civilizations, such as the Mayans, Egyptians, and Tibetans—each of whom carried similar wisdom, suggesting that yoga's roots spread far beyond India.

Shiva, as the Adi Yogi, was the origin of all yogic wisdom. He showed the complete path to human liberation.

The Saptarishis, though each specializing in a unique aspect, received and carried forth this wisdom. They are the first spiritual scientists of humanity. Their teachings became the foundation of countless spiritual paths, shaping the course of human civilization.

Where Did Yoga Begin?

Yoga, in its truest form, began in ancient India, long before formal religions like Hinduism and Buddhism took shape. Its roots can be traced to the **Vedas**, the oldest sacred texts in India.

Yoga was later systematized and further explained in revered texts like:

- **The Yoga Sutras of Patanjali** (a practical guide to the science of yoga),
- **The Bhagavad Gita** (a profound philosophical dialogue on duty and devotion),
- **The Upanishads** (explorations into the nature of consciousness and the self).

These texts were not just religious writings—they were manuals for exploring the inner world, written by those who had mastered it through direct experience.

So, Who Is a Yogi?

A true yogi is not defined by their ability to contort their body into intricate postures. Rather, a yogi is someone who has transcended the limitations of the mind, overcome the ego, and touched something beyond the individual self—something universal and timeless.

A yogi can be anyone who walks the path of self-awareness:

- A monk in the Himalayas, in silent communion with the divine,
- A scientist unraveling the mysteries of consciousness,
- Or anyone who consciously chooses awareness over mindless existence.

Learning about Adi Yogi and the ancient origins of yoga led me to a profound realization:

I don't need to become someone I'm not to walk this path. I simply need to become more of who I already am.

Yoga wasn't conceived as a religion—it was born as a journey inward, a journey to explore and align with the deepest truths of existence.

CHAPTER 9
HOW GODS CAME INTO HINDUISM?

In the yogic tradition, Shiva is revered not simply as a "God" in the conventional sense, but as the Adi Yogi (The First Yogi) and Adi Guru (The First Guru) — the one who introduced the science of yoga to the Saptarishis, the seven ancient sages. This is not mythology in the traditional sense, but rather a record of yogic history — a spiritual process that predates organized religion.

The Saptarishis, who were the original recipients of this sacred knowledge, then carried this profound wisdom across the world, planting the seeds of yogic science in cultures far beyond the Indian subcontinent. This knowledge, based on direct inner experience, became the foundation of what we now call yogic science — a practice rooted not in belief systems but in personal, transformative experience.

As the millennia passed, what began as a pure, experiential science — Sanatana Dharma (The Eternal Way) — gradually evolved into a system of spiritual expression. The deep, esoteric truths of yoga were transmitted through symbolism, stories, and devotional practices, making them more accessible to the common people. This marked the beginning of what we recognize today as the Hindu pantheon.

Deities as Archetypes of Inner Qualities:

In this evolving system, the deities were not simply external gods to be worshipped, but rather archetypal representations of inner qualities and cosmic principles:

- **Shiva** became the symbol of stillness, the destruction of ignorance, and the transcendence of the mind through meditation.

- ○ **Vishnu** embodied balance, preservation, and the upholding of dharma (cosmic law).
- ○ **Brahma** represented the creative intelligence and the force behind the unfolding of the universe.
- ○ **Devi (Shakti)** personified the divine feminine energy, the dynamic force that empowers creation itself.

Mythology as a Bridge to the Divine:

The Vedas and the Puranas began to articulate stories about these deities, not as external, distant beings, but as symbolic representations of cosmic principles. These stories were not mere folklore; they were designed to communicate deep spiritual truths, often encoded in metaphor, inviting the seeker to engage with them on a personal level.

For those unable to sit in deep meditation like a yogi, the Bhakti path (the path of devotion) offered a way to connect to the divine through love, surrender, and ritual. Bhakti Yoga allowed individuals to express their devotion and experience spiritual growth through worship and heartfelt connection.

From Yogic Science to Religion

To understand the transformation from yogic science to religious practice, it helps to recognize the difference between the three:

- ○ **Yogic Science**: The direct experience of inner truth through meditation, awareness, and self-realization — a practical technology for inner transformation.
- ○ **Spiritual Symbolism**: The gods and goddesses as tools for self-realization — symbolic representations of aspects of the inner self that guide the practitioner toward higher states of consciousness.

- **Religion**: Over time, these symbolic teachings were formalized into culturally shaped systems of belief and worship, becoming institutionalized and often fixed in ritual practices.

As the centuries passed, the profound and transformative nature of yogic science began to get lost. Mythological stories, once intended to convey deep inner truths, were often taken as literal historical accounts, and the spiritual tools (gods, rituals, practices) began to be worshipped for their own sake. This divergence marked the beginning of religion as we know it today, distinct from the core teachings of yogic realization.

So, What's the Deeper Truth?

The ancient yogis understood something fundamental:

"What you call Shiva, Vishnu, or Devi are not gods up in the heavens, but dimensions of your own consciousness."

In this light, the gods are not external beings separate from us, but gateways to explore the vast, infinite landscape of our own inner cosmos. They are reflections of the infinite intelligence within us all. Far from being imaginary figures, they embody the divine principles we each carry within, waiting to be awakened.

Timeline: The Evolution from Yogic Science to Religion

1. Pre-Vedic Age – The Yogic Beginnings

Shiva as Adiyogi: The First Yogi

In the earliest dawn of yogic knowledge, Shiva stands as the Adiyogi — the First Yogi, a figure of profound stillness, immersed in deep meditation at Mount Kailash. It is here that he enters a state of perfect union with the cosmos, embodying the pinnacle of yogic realization.

Transmission to the Saptarishis

Shiva's wisdom, not merely theory but the living experience of ultimate truth, is passed on to the Saptarishis (The Seven Sages). These sages, who had dedicated themselves to inner discovery, became the first disciples of this ancient science, receiving teachings on self-mastery, consciousness, and the nature of existence itself.

Yogic Science Spreads Across the Ancient World

With deep reverence for their new knowledge, the Saptarishis traveled far and wide — from what is now India to the lands of Mesopotamia, Egypt, and beyond — sharing the experiential science of consciousness, body, breath, and mind. This was not mere philosophy, but a practice rooted in direct experience, and it began to shape civilizations around the world.

Focus: Inner realization, direct experience, meditation, and self-mastery.

2. Vedic Period (~1500 BCE and earlier) – Sound as Creation

The Vedas: Heard, Not Written

The Vedic period marks a critical juncture in the evolution of yogic wisdom. The Vedas, sacred texts composed in deep meditative states, were not written by human hands but were heard directly by the Rishis (seers) during their spiritual practice. These revelations were of such depth that they transcended the mundane world, offering insights into the nature of the universe and existence.

The Gods as Forces of Nature

During this time, gods such as Indra, Agni, Varuna, and Soma were understood not as anthropomorphic beings, but as cosmic forces— manifestations of the natural elements and inner energies of life. These divine forces were not separate from creation but were interwoven with the very fabric of existence.

Rituals as Pathways to Cosmic Harmony

Rituals, or yajnas, were performed to invoke these forces, utilizing sacred mantras and fire as mediums for connection with the cosmos. In essence, the Vedic rituals were a way of harmonizing with the natural order through the use of sacred sound and fire, bridging the human realm with the divine.

Focus: Harmonizing with nature and cosmic forces through mantra, fire, and sacred sound.

3. Upanishadic Age (~800 BCE onwards) – The Inner Shift

Philosophical Inquiry: "Who Am I?"

With the dawn of the Upanishads, a new wave of deep philosophical inquiry took center stage. Seers and sages began to ask the essential questions of existence: "Who am I?" and "What is Brahman?" These texts, which explore the nature of self and the cosmos, marked a profound shift from external ritual to internal realization.

Emergence of Atman and Brahman

The Atman (individual soul) and Brahman (the cosmic self) became central to the Upanishadic teachings. The realization emerged that the divine was not external but inherent within — "Tat Tvam Asi" ("You are That"), the core truth that the individual soul is one with the universal spirit.

Focus: Self-realization, transcendence, subtle body, consciousness.

4. Puranic Era (~300 BCE – 1000 CE) – Stories and Symbols

The Rise of Mythology

The Puranic era witnessed a shift in how yogic wisdom was transmitted. Mythological stories, found in texts like the Bhagavatam, Shiva Purana, and Devi Purana, began to take on greater importance. These stories brought the gods, such as Shiva, Vishnu, Krishna, Rama, and Durga, into more humanized forms, with their divine attributes being more relatable to the masses.

Temples and the Bhakti Movement

Temples began to be built, and the Bhakti movement (the path of devotion) flourished. For those who could not access the inner practices of meditation, devotion became a powerful path to the divine. Through love, surrender, and ritual, devotees could connect with the gods and receive divine blessings.

Focus: Symbolic stories to help the masses relate to the divine. Inner truths veiled in mythology.

5. Tantric & Siddha Traditions (Parallel Timeline)

The Quest for Mastery over Energy

While the Vedic and Upanishadic traditions were developing, a parallel spiritual stream was flourishing — the Tantric and Siddha traditions. In the

Tamil lands, the Siddhars and in the Himalayas, the Tantrics explored the profound mysteries of the body, breath, energy, and the subtle body. These traditions were not concerned with abstract philosophy but with the practical science of transforming one's energy.

Energy as the Key to Immortality

In these traditions, practices centered around mastering the chakras, nadis, mantras, and the very flow of life energy. The ultimate goal was not just spiritual realization but the mastery of the physical and energetic body, often referred to as kaya siddhi, or the attainment of physical immortality.

Focus: Energy transformation, inner alchemy, sacred geometry, living temples.

6. Modern Hinduism (Post 1000 CE) – Religion Becomes Dominant

The Shift from Inner Knowledge to External Worship

As time passed, the gods began to be seen less as symbols of inner qualities and more as external beings to be worshipped literally. Caste structures, temple hierarchies, and ritualistic practices took center stage. The core yogic teachings, once deeply rooted in inner science, began to fade from the collective consciousness.

Focus: Devotion, ritual, cultural identity — but often lacking the depth of yogic realization unless one chooses to dive deeper.

7. The Return to Inner Science (Present Time)

A Modern Resurgence

In the present age, a growing number of seekers are returning to the roots of the yogic tradition. There is a rediscovery of the inner science behind the symbols and rituals. More people are coming to understand that Shiva is not a deity outside of us, but a possibility within each of us.

Mantras, Mudras, and Practices as Technologies of the Inner World

The ancient practices — from mantras and mudras to meditation and breathwork — are no longer seen as superstition or blind faith, but as powerful tools for inner transformation and spiritual evolution.

The deities were never meant to be external entities. They are reflections of the inner cosmos, facets of the self that are accessible to anyone willing to embark on the journey of self-realization. The true religion is not in outward worship, but in turning inward to discover who we truly are. Whether through yoga, tantra, or devotion, all paths ultimately lead to the realization that **"You Are That"** — the divine, the eternal, the infinite.

Understanding the Divine in Yogic Tradition

In the rich and intricate tapestry of Hinduism, the many gods are not viewed as separate and distinct supreme beings but rather as manifestations of the Divine itself, each symbolizing specific energies, purposes, and spiritual processes. These deities are not to be worshipped blindly or with literal belief, but understood as tools for inner transformation, each offering a unique pathway to higher states of consciousness.

Here's a deeper exploration of what these deities represent:

1. Gods as Energies, Not Personalities

In the yogic tradition, gods like Vishnu, Devi, Ganesha, Muruga, and others are not merely figures from mythology. They are personified energies, embodiments of universal principles, and tools for inner growth. They serve as focal points for spiritual evolution, offering wisdom, protection, and guidance along the journey of self-discovery.

"In this culture, we did not look up and invent gods. We looked inward and realized divine possibilities."

The gods, then, are not external figures to be revered in isolation, but internal archetypes—representations of different energies within us, guiding us to explore deeper realms of existence.

2. Shiva as the Adi Yogi – The Source of Yogic Science

Shiva, in yogic understanding, is not a "god" in the conventional religious sense but is revered as the Adi Yogi, the first yogi—the originator of yoga itself. He embodies the primordial state of stillness and consciousness, the foundation from which all spiritual practices emerge.

While other gods represent specific aspects of creation, Shiva's essence transcends them. He is the godhead, the source of yogic wisdom. His teachings and practices are the foundation of all spiritual paths. The other gods are seen as manifestations of various cosmic principles suited for different human needs and temperaments.

- **Vishnu:** The Preserver of life and cosmic order.
- **Brahma:** The creator principle, though not actively worshipped, for creation is ever-ongoing.
- **Devi (Shakti):** The dynamic energy (Prakriti) that fuels creation.
- **Ganesha:** The intelligence that removes obstacles.
- **Muruga/Kartikeya:** The embodiment of ultimate knowledge and inner courage.

3. Gods as Technologies for Transformation

In the yogic culture of India, gods were not created for mere belief. Instead, they were designed as technologies for well-being—spiritual tools meant to guide individuals towards inner liberation.

Temples, rituals, and deities are seen as mechanisms or methods to connect with subtler dimensions of existence. They are not idols to be worshipped mindlessly, but representations of spiritual technologies that aid in the deepening of one's connection to the divine within.

"In India, we didn't create gods for belief, we created them as technologies for wellbeing."

4. No Conflict with Multiple Gods

The diversity of gods in Hinduism reflects the profound richness of the inner human experience. It's not polytheism in the Western sense, but rather a scientific approach to exploring the infinite facets of the One Source. Each deity represents a unique dimension of the cosmic reality, and rather than competing, they complement one another.

"Shiva is not a god, he is the godhead — the very source of yogic sciences. The others—Vishnu, Devi, Ganesha—are not in competition with Shiva. They are various expressions of the same ultimate reality, suited for different human needs and temperaments."

"In this culture, we created 33 million gods—not to confuse people, but to offer every individual a doorway to the divine, in a form they can relate to."

Thus, these deities are not objects of blind belief, but keys to inner exploration. The gods are doors to higher consciousness, each tailored to different aspects of human life.

A Yogic and Symbolic Breakdown of Key Deities in the Indian Spiritual Tradition

These deities are not to be seen as gods to worship in the traditional sense, but as inner archetypes or cosmic principles, each representing a unique energy or aspect of the self. Here's a deeper look into their symbolic and yogic significance:

1. Shiva – The Adi yogi (The First Yogi)

Yogic Meaning: Shiva embodies stillness, absolute consciousness, and the potential for transformation. He represents Tamas—the quiet potential from which everything arises.

Symbolism:

- **Third Eye**: Represents awareness and perception beyond ordinary sight.
- **Crescent Moon**: Mastery over time and cyclical life.
- **Snakes**: Power over death and fear, representing the transcendence of mortality.
- **Sitting in Meditation**: Symbolizes the ultimate state of inner stillness and detachment.
- **Inner Archetype**: For those walking the path of self-realization, Shiva represents the ultimate yogi—the one who has gone beyond.

2. Vishnu – The Preserver

Yogic Meaning: Vishnu represents Sattva, the quality of balance, harmony, and preservation of cosmic order (Dharma).

Symbolism:

Conch: Symbolizes the sound of the universe, the primal vibration.

Discus: Represents the mind, which must be mastered for balance.

Blue Skin: Indicates the infinite nature of his being, as vast as the sky.

Inner Archetype: For those focused on maintaining order and harmony, Vishnu's energy guides the balance necessary for life.

3. Devi (Durga, Kali, Parvati, etc.) – The Divine Feminine

Yogic Meaning: Devi represents Shakti, the primordial energy that is the driving force behind all creation and evolution.

Symbolism:

- **Weapons**: Represent inner strength and the ability to overcome obstacles.
- **Tiger/Lion**: Represents the wild nature that is tamed through spiritual discipline.
- **Multiple Hands**: Symbolizes omnipotence, the capacity to handle many dimensions of existence simultaneously.
- **Inner Archetype**: Devi embodies the power to awaken deep courage, strength, and compassion within oneself.

4. Ganesha – The Remover of Obstacles

Yogic Meaning: Ganesha symbolizes intelligence grounded in awareness, serving as the gatekeeper to deeper spiritual experiences.

Symbolism:

- **Elephant Head**: Represents wisdom and memory.
- **Big Ears**: Symbolizes the capacity for deep listening and mindfulness.

- ◦ **Broken Tusk**: Represents the sacrifice necessary to overcome one's own limitations.
- ◦ **Inner Archetype**: Before any inner work or external task, Ganesha's energy represents the removal of mental and karmic obstacles.

5. Hanuman – The Devotee and Supreme Strength

Yogic Meaning: Hanuman embodies Bhakti (devotion), Seva (selfless service), and the strength used with humility.

Symbolism:

- ◦ **Monkey Face**: Represents the mind, which must be mastered to unlock true potential.
- ◦ **Tail**: Symbolizes Kundalini energy, the dormant spiritual power within.
- ◦ **Devotion to Rama**: Illustrates selfless surrender to the divine.
- ◦ **Inner Archetype**: For those walking the path of love and service, Hanuman embodies the ideal—a figure who is unshakable, fearless, and full of energy.

6. Lord Murugan – The Symbol of Wisdom and Transformation

In Tamil yogic traditions, Murugan (also known as Skanda, Karthikeya, and Subramanya) is not merely a deity but a profound symbol of supreme wisdom and the ideal guru.

- ◦ **Six Faces (Arumugam)**: Represent the six dimensions of perception or the six chakras, leading to the seventh—enlightenment.
- ◦ **Vel (Divine Spear)**: The piercing clarity of knowledge, which cuts through ignorance (Avidya).
- ◦ **Peacock (Vehicle)**: Symbolizes the mind when it is tamed and becomes a servant to the soul.

- ○ **Rooster on Flag**: Represents the transcendence of ego, not through suppression, but through victory over it.
- ○ **Born from Shiva's Third Eye**: Wisdom arises from the inner eye—the awakened awareness, not from the external senses.

Murugan is often revered as the master of Kundalini, the inner fire, and the embodiment of ultimate wisdom. His battle with Surapadman is not mere mythology but an allegory for conquering inner demons—fear, doubt, and ego.

"Murugan is not a war god. He is the fire of wisdom that burns away your ignorance." — Yogic Insight

In yogic science, these deities are not to be worshipped blindly. They are tools—each one pointing to a different aspect of the self or the cosmos. They are keys to unlocking the deepest dimensions of inner knowing and transformation. **"You don't have to believe in a god. You have to become one—aware, conscious, and boundless."**

CHAPTER 10
THE BHAGAVAD GITA

The Bhagavad Gita, often referred to as the "Song of God," is a timeless spiritual and philosophical text. It unfolds as a profound dialogue between Lord Krishna and his disciple Arjuna during the tumultuous battle of Kurukshetra. The Gita's 18 chapters, known as Adhyayas, serve as a detailed exploration of human existence, ethics, spirituality, and the path to self-realization. Each chapter offers a unique perspective on life's challenges, and Krishna's teachings are designed to guide Arjuna—and humanity—through the complexities of the material and spiritual worlds.

Here's an overview of the 18 chapters of the Bhagavad Gita:

1. Arjuna Vishada Yoga – The Yoga of Arjuna's Dejection

Summary:

The opening chapter sets the stage for the dialogue between Krishna and Arjuna. Arjuna, a warrior of immense skill, is consumed by moral conflict and emotional turmoil as he faces the prospect of fighting against his own kin, teachers, and friends on the battlefield. Overcome with sorrow, compassion, and confusion, he is unable to make a decision, caught in a deep moral crisis. This chapter introduces Arjuna's inner struggle, which becomes the catalyst for the spiritual teachings that follow.

2. Sankhya Yoga – The Yoga of Knowledge

Summary:

In this pivotal chapter, Krishna begins his discourse with Arjuna on the nature of the soul (Atman). Krishna explains the distinction between the physical body and the eternal soul, emphasizing that the soul is imperishable, while the body is transient. He introduces Sankhya, the yoga of knowledge, which teaches the path of discerning wisdom. Krishna urges Arjuna to act selflessly, without attachment to the results, and to recognize that true spiritual practice lies in understanding one's deeper nature.

3. Karma Yoga – The Yoga of Selfless Action

Summary:

Here, Krishna emphasizes the concept of Karma Yoga, the path of selfless action. He teaches Arjuna that one must fulfill their duties without attachment to the results, as actions performed with attachment bind the soul to the cycle of karma. By acting selflessly, one can purify the mind and attain spiritual freedom. This chapter highlights the essential principle of duty (dharma) and how performing one's role in life without personal desire leads to liberation.

4. Jnana Karma Sanyasa Yoga – The Yoga of Knowledge and Renunciation of Action

Summary:

Krishna reveals the interconnection between knowledge and action, explaining that spiritual wisdom can transform the way one engages in the world. Actions, when performed in alignment with spiritual wisdom, lead to liberation. Krishna also teaches that renunciation is not the abandonment of physical activity but the renunciation of attachment to the fruits of one's actions.

5. Karma Sanyasa Yoga – The Yoga of Renunciation of Action

Summary:

In this chapter, Krishna elaborates further on Karma Sanyasa, the renunciation of actions performed with selfish desires. He clarifies that true renunciation is not about withdrawing from the world, but about renouncing ego-driven attachment to the outcomes of action. This chapter explores the balance between action and renunciation, emphasizing that selfless action, coupled with detachment, leads to spiritual liberation.

6. Dhyana Yoga – The Yoga of Meditation

Summary:

Krishna introduces the path of Dhyana Yoga, the yoga of meditation, focusing on the importance of mental discipline, self-control, and concentration. He explains how meditation leads to inner peace and union with the divine. Krishna emphasizes that a disciplined mind is essential for spiritual progress, and regular meditation allows the seeker to experience a direct connection with higher consciousness.

7. Jnana Vijnana Yoga – The Yoga of Knowledge and Wisdom

Summary:

In this chapter, Krishna reveals deeper truths about divine knowledge (Jnana) and wisdom (Vijnana). He explains the relationship between the material and spiritual worlds and reveals the nature of the divine. Krishna emphasizes that true devotion to God leads to enlightenment and liberation, and that this wisdom transforms one's understanding of life, leading to the realization of the Self.

8. Aksara Brahma Yoga – The Yoga of the Imperishable Absolute

Summary:

Krishna delves into the concept of Aksara Brahman, the imperishable absolute reality. He teaches that while the material world is impermanent, the soul is eternal. Krishna explains the journey of the soul after death, illustrating that spiritual practice is the key to attaining union with the divine and escaping the cycle of birth and death. This chapter highlights the significance of spiritual practice and devotion as the means to transcend the limitations of time.

9. Raja Vidya Raja Guhya Yoga – The Yoga of Royal Knowledge and Royal Secret

Summary:

Krishna unveils the royal knowledge and royal secret, the highest forms of spiritual wisdom. He teaches that surrender to God and devotion to the Divine are the ultimate paths to liberation. Krishna emphasizes the transformative power of Bhakti Yoga, the path of love and devotion, and how it leads to union with the divine.

10. Vibhuti Yoga – The Yoga of Divine Glories

Summary:

In this chapter, Krishna reveals his many divine manifestations (Vibhuti) throughout the universe. He describes how the divine expresses itself through all forms of life, natural phenomena, and cosmic processes. Krishna explains that everything in the universe is a reflection of the divine, and by recognizing these manifestations, one can deepen their understanding of God's omnipresence.

11. Visvarupa Darshana Yoga – The Yoga of the Vision of the Universal Form

Summary:

Krishna grants Arjuna the divine vision to witness his universal form (Visvarupa)—a cosmic, all-encompassing manifestation that transcends the physical realm. Arjuna beholds the infinite nature of Krishna, which is both awe-inspiring and terrifying. This chapter highlights the vastness of divine reality and reveals the interconnectedness of all existence.

12. Bhakti Yoga – The Yoga of Devotion

Summary:

This chapter focuses on the path of Bhakti Yoga, the yoga of devotion. Krishna explains that sincere love and devotion to God are the highest means of attaining spiritual fulfillment and liberation. He describes the qualities of a true devotee and the transformative power of devotion, emphasizing that devotion is the ultimate expression of the soul's love for the Divine.

13. Kshetra Kshetragna Vibhaga Yoga – The Yoga of the Field and the Knower of the Field

Summary:

Krishna explains the distinction between the physical body (the "field") and the eternal soul (the "knower of the field"). He teaches that the soul is unaffected by the material world, and understanding this truth is key to overcoming illusion (Maya) and realizing the true nature of the self.

14. Gunatraya Vibhaga Yoga – The Yoga of the Division of the Three Gunas

Summary:

Krishna elaborates on the three Gunas (qualities of nature): Sattva (goodness), Rajas (passion), and Tamas (ignorance). He explains how these qualities influence human behavior and perceptions. Krishna guides Arjuna on how to transcend these qualities to attain spiritual liberation and rise above the forces of nature.

15. Purushottama Yoga – The Yoga of the Supreme Divine Personality

Summary:

In this chapter, Krishna reveals his true identity as the Supreme Divine Personality (Purushottama), beyond all gods and spiritual beings. He explains the nature of the eternal soul and the relationship between the material and spiritual worlds. The chapter emphasizes the ultimate reality of God and the path to union with the Supreme Divine.

16. Daivasura Sampad Vibhaga Yoga – The Yoga of the Division between the Divine and the Demonic

Summary:

Krishna contrasts the divine and demonic qualities within human beings. He describes the divine attributes of purity, compassion, and self-control, and the demonic traits of greed, anger, and delusion. Krishna teaches that one's actions, thoughts, and desires shape their spiritual destiny and influence their progress toward liberation.

17. Shraddhatraya Vibhaga Yoga – The Yoga of the Three Divisions of Faith

Summary:

This chapter explores the nature of faith and how it is influenced by the three Gunas. Krishna explains that different types of faith lead to different kinds of actions and spiritual outcomes. He stresses the importance of cultivating pure, sattvic faith for true spiritual growth.

18. Moksha Sanyasa Yoga – The Yoga of Liberation and Renunciation

Summary:

The final chapter of the Gita consolidates all the teachings and focuses on Moksha—the ultimate goal of liberation from the cycle of birth and death. Krishna emphasizes that freedom is achieved through selfless action, devotion, and the realization of the true nature of the self. He guides Arjuna to renounce the ego and act with full devotion to attain spiritual liberation.

The Bhagavad Gita is not just a scripture—it is a timeless manual for life, offering profound wisdom for overcoming inner conflicts and realizing one's true divine nature. The teachings of Krishna continue to inspire seekers on the path of truth, knowledge, and selfless service.

CHAPTER 11
THE TIMELESS TEACHINGS OF THE BHAGAVAD GITA AND THEIR RESONANCE IN YOGIC WISDOM

The timeless wisdom of the Bhagavad Gita aligns deeply with the profound teachings passed down by yogis throughout history. These teachings have often centered on understanding the nature of the self, the universe, and the very fabric of reality. The principles found in the Gita, such as selfless action, meditation, detachment, and devotion, are not only universal but have been the cornerstone of yogic philosophy and practice for millennia. Yogis, as spiritual seekers, have consistently explored the depths of these themes, and their teachings mirror the essence of what Krishna imparts to Arjuna in the Gita.

In this exploration, we will see how the timeless wisdom of the Gita is reflected in the practices of yogis — transmitted through oral traditions and sacred texts — and how the path of yoga serves as a living expression of these teachings, guiding seekers toward spiritual realization.

1. The Nature of the Self (Atman)

At the heart of yogic wisdom is the understanding that our true essence is eternal and beyond the physical body. In the Bhagavad Gita, Krishna teaches Arjuna that the Atman, or soul, is indestructible. It transcends birth and death, and cannot be harmed by physical forces. This teaching echoes the deep wisdom of yogis, who have long understood that the body is but a temporary vessel, while the true self is eternal.

Example from Yogis: In Patanjali's Yoga Sutras, the nature of the self is explored through the lens of self-realization. In verse 1.3, Patanjali states,

"Yoga is the cessation of the fluctuations of the mind." This powerful insight reveals that when we quiet the mind through practices like meditation, we can experience our true self — the Atman, which is beyond the distractions of the physical world. The yogic goal is not merely to control the mind, but to reach a state of awareness where we can directly experience our divine nature, which is eternal and free.

2. Detachment and Selfless Action (Karma Yoga)

A central teaching of the Gita is the practice of Karma Yoga — the art of selfless action performed without attachment to the fruits of one's labor. Krishna instructs Arjuna to act in accordance with his dharma (righteous duty), but without concern for the outcome. This teaching, one of the pillars of the Gita, is echoed by yogis throughout history, who emphasize the importance of performing actions with purity and intention, but without being bound by the results.

Example from Yogis: In the Jivanmuktiviveka, a text that elaborates the teachings of Advaita Vedanta (non-duality), the great sage Adi Shankaracharya emphasizes the value of living in the world and fulfilling one's duties, but without attachment to outcomes. Similarly, yogis like Sri Ramakrishna taught that selfless service (Seva) is an embodiment of Karma Yoga. The act of giving without expectation of return frees the heart and mind, allowing the soul to move closer to liberation. Through such practice, the ego is transcended, and true freedom emerges.

3. Meditation and the Nature of Reality (Dhyana Yoga)

Krishna speaks to Arjuna about the importance of Dhyana Yoga, the yoga of meditation, as a means of purifying the mind and achieving clarity and spiritual insight. Meditation, or mental discipline, is central to yogic practices, and it is through the cultivation of concentration and focus that we can awaken to the higher self.

Example from Yogis: Swami Sivananda, one of the most revered modern yogis, often emphasized the importance of meditation as a direct means of connecting with the higher self. In his book The Practice of Meditation, Swami Sivananda describes meditation as the key to stilling the mind, enabling the practitioner to transcend the ego and experience the unity of all existence. Similarly, Sri Sri Ravi Shankar, the founder of the Art of Living Foundation, teaches that through practices like Sudarshan Kriya and other forms of meditation, the mind can be silenced, allowing one to experience the divine presence that resides within.

4. Knowledge and Wisdom (Jnana Yoga)

The Bhagavad Gita teaches the path of Jnana Yoga, the yoga of knowledge, where Krishna encourages Arjuna to understand the nature of the self and the universe in order to achieve liberation. Self-inquiry is central to this path, which involves questioning the nature of existence and realizing the deeper truths about reality.

Example from Yogis: Ramana Maharshi, one of the most profound yogis of the modern age, centered his teachings on the practice of Atma Vichara (self-inquiry). His question, "Who am I?", was not a rhetorical one but a deep and direct probe into the nature of the self. This constant questioning leads to the direct realization of the Atman, or true self. Similarly, the ancient Upanishads, foundational texts for yogic philosophy, offer profound insights into the nature of reality. The Isha Upanishad, for example, speaks of realizing the divine in everything and perceiving the self as one with the entire universe — much like the wisdom Krishna shares in the Gita.

5. Devotion and Surrender (Bhakti Yoga)

Krishna emphasizes the path of Bhakti Yoga, the yoga of devotion, in the Gita. He teaches that surrendering to the divine with pure love and devotion is the key to attaining liberation. Bhakti, or devotional love, is a transformative practice that helps transcend the ego and connects the soul with the divine.

Example from Yogis: Swami Vivekananda, a prominent disciple of Ramakrishna, often spoke of Bhakti Yoga as the path of love and surrender. He taught that by offering everything — desires, ego, and attachments — to the divine, one could transcend the limitations of the self and discover a higher purpose. The practice of chanting mantras, or engaging in kirtan (devotional singing), is central to the Bhakti tradition. This sacred music, prayer, and ritual allow the devotee to express love for the divine and experience spiritual unity.

6. The Role of the Guru (Spiritual Teacher)

The Guru plays a pivotal role in both the Bhagavad Gita and in the lives of yogis. Krishna himself acts as Arjuna's guru, guiding him with wisdom and offering counsel during moments of confusion. Similarly, in yogic traditions, the guru is seen as a necessary guide, helping the seeker navigate the challenges of the spiritual path and leading them to the realization of their true self.

Example from Yogis: Sri Ramakrishna taught that the guru is essential for spiritual growth, helping to clear the obstacles of the mind. Without the guidance of a realized teacher, the seeker may become lost in the complexities of the mind. Likewise, Swami Sivananda frequently spoke of the need for a spiritual teacher to help the seeker on the path of self-realization.

7. Liberation (Moksha)

The ultimate goal in both the Bhagavad Gita and yogic philosophy is Moksha, liberation from the cycle of birth and death (samsara). Moksha is the state of union with the divine and the realization of one's essential nature as pure consciousness.

Example from Yogis: Sri Aurobindo described Moksha as a state of union with the divine, where the individual soul transcends all limitations and merges into the infinite consciousness. Similarly, yogis like Swami Dayananda Saraswati taught that liberation is achieved through self-realization and merging with the divine essence that pervades all of existence.

The profound teachings of the Bhagavad Gita resonate deeply with the yogic traditions passed down through the ages. These teachings — self-realization, detachment, devotion, and the pursuit of spiritual freedom — have been expressed in various forms by yogis throughout history. Whether through meditation, selfless action, knowledge, or devotion, the yogic path aligns seamlessly with the wisdom of the Gita, guiding seekers toward unity with the universe, the discovery of their true self, and the transcendence of the ego to experience the divine. In essence, both the Gita and the yogic teachings offer a roadmap for a life of awakening, where one realizes their oneness with the divine and the eternal truth of existence.

CHAPTER 12
KARMA & DHARMA - HOW ACTIONS AND INNER TENDENCIES SHAPE EXPERIENCE

As I journeyed deeper into the spiritual path, the concepts of Karma and Dharma slowly revealed themselves to me, not as mere intellectual ideas, but as living, breathing forces shaping our reality. The more I meditated on them, the more I saw how they were intricately woven into the very fabric of our lives — our choices, our relationships, our experiences — all were shaped by these two cosmic laws.

I once believed that karma was simply the idea that our actions come back to us in some way — a kind of cosmic retribution. Dharma, on the other hand, seemed to be a set of moral codes or duties we had to follow. But as I continued to delve into these teachings, I began to see the depth, beauty, and complexity of both. They weren't separate concepts; they were deeply connected — karma and dharma were two sides of the same coin, influencing the unfolding of our lives, guiding us toward our highest potential, and helping us understand the deeper meaning behind our experiences.

The Law of Karma: The Seeds We Sow

The word karma is often misunderstood. It is not punishment or reward, but simply the law of cause and effect. Every thought, word, and action we take creates an imprint — a samskara — on our subtle body, which influences future experiences. Just as a seed grows into a plant, each action we take plants the seed for future outcomes. These seeds are not always harvested immediately; they may sprout in this lifetime, or they may wait for many lifetimes to come.

Karma is not a cosmic scoreboard, keeping track of our good and bad actions, but a subtle energy, a vibration that shapes our lives according to our choices. When we act with intention and awareness, we create positive karma, bringing us closer to peace, joy, and spiritual growth. When we act with ignorance, attachment, or hatred, we sow seeds of suffering, which may manifest in future circumstances.

In the Bhagavad Gita, Krishna speaks about karma as the need for action without attachment to the fruits of that action. He encourages us to perform our duties without expectation, to surrender the outcome, and to act in accordance with our highest self.

The beauty of karma lies in its transformative power — as we begin to live with awareness and mindfulness, we have the ability to purify our past karmic imprints and choose actions that lead us toward liberation. Every act of love, every act of selflessness, every moment of awareness burns away the seeds of past karma, transforming them into something new, something higher.

Dharma: The Unique Path of the Soul

While karma is the imprint left by our past actions, dharma is the unique path that each of us must follow in this life. It is not a prescribed set of rules or duties given by society, but rather the soul's calling — the inner compass guiding us back to our true nature. Dharma is a dynamic and evolving path that aligns us with our essence, helping us fulfill our highest potential.

Each of us has a unique dharma — a purpose, a role in the world, that resonates deeply with our innermost being. This dharma is not dictated by external society or circumstances, but by our internal alignment with truth, love, and wisdom. Our dharma evolves over time, shifting with the stages of life and the inner growth we experience.

In the great epics of India, Mahabharata and Ramayana, the concept of dharma is explored in depth, with characters constantly grappling with the question: What is my duty? What is the right action?

Dharma in the Mahabharata: Arjuna's Dilemma

One of the most profound teachings of dharma comes from the Mahabharata. Arjuna, the great warrior, is faced with a moral and spiritual dilemma on the battlefield of Kurukshetra. He stands at the precipice of war, unsure whether he should fight in the battle against his family and beloved teachers, or whether he should renounce the violence of war altogether. His heart is torn, as he is uncertain of the right path.

At this moment of inner turmoil, Lord Krishna speaks to Arjuna, offering the wisdom of dharma. He explains that it is Arjuna's dharma, as a Kshatriya (warrior class), to fight in the battle — not out of personal desire or revenge, but as an act of selfless duty to protect righteousness (dharma) and preserve the cosmic order (rta). Krishna reveals to Arjuna that his actions must be aligned with his higher purpose, not driven by the ego's desires or fears. It is this selfless action, performed in alignment with dharma, that leads to true liberation.

Arjuna's journey reflects our own struggles in life — the constant battle between the desires of the ego and the higher callings of the soul. Just as Arjuna must discern his duty from his own inner wisdom, we too must seek to understand our own unique dharma — the path we must walk to fulfill our highest potential and align with our true purpose.

Dharma in the Ramayana: Lord Rama's Unwavering Integrity

The Ramayana offers another beautiful example of dharma, through the life and actions of Lord Rama. Rama, born as the seventh incarnation of Vishnu, embodies the principles of dharma in every aspect of his life. He is the perfect man, the ideal son, the ideal husband, and the ideal king. His life is a reflection of living in perfect harmony with the laws of the universe.

When Rama is exiled to the forest, he chooses to honor his father's promise, despite the personal pain it causes him. He acts with unwavering integrity, knowing that his actions, guided by dharma, are the path to inner peace and alignment with the cosmic order. Even when faced with the greatest challenges — such as rescuing his wife, Sita, from the demon king Ravana — Rama continues to act with righteousness, humility, and devotion to his higher calling.

Through Rama, we see that dharma is not just about following societal rules or fulfilling external duties; it is about aligning our actions with our inner truth, no matter how difficult the circumstances. It is the courage to stand firm in our values and to follow our soul's purpose, regardless of the external pressures or challenges we face.

The Interplay of Karma and Dharma

As I reflect on these stories, I see how the concepts of karma and dharma are intertwined. Our past actions (karma) shape our present circumstances, and our present choices (dharma) will create the future we experience. The path of dharma is not always clear, and it often requires us to transcend the limitations of our past karma — to rise above the conditioning of the mind and ego — in order to act in alignment with our higher purpose.

Living in accordance with dharma requires courage, self-awareness, and deep inner wisdom. It requires us to listen to the subtle whispers of the soul, to discern the path that will bring us into alignment with the highest good.

At times, this path may lead us through struggles and suffering, as it did for both Arjuna and Rama, but it is only through such trials that we can purify our karma and grow closer to the truth of who we really are.

The Sacred Dance of Karma and Dharma

In this dance of karma and dharma, we are not passive observers, but active participants in the unfolding of our lives. We are constantly shaping our reality through the choices we make, and those choices are guided by the energy of our past actions and the calling of our soul. As we begin to act with awareness, aligning our actions with our highest truth, we step into the flow of dharma — the sacred dance of life.

It is a journey of self-discovery, of understanding that every experience, every moment, every encounter is a reflection of our own karma, and every action we take is an opportunity to live in alignment with dharma. And in this dance, we come to understand that life is not something to be controlled or fixed, but something to be embraced, moment by moment, with full awareness and love.

The eternal play of karma and dharma continues, as the soul evolves, learns, and grows — forever moving toward the ultimate goal of liberation, of union with the divine.

As I walk this path, I realize that dharma is not about reaching a destination — it is the journey itself. The choices we make, the actions we take, and the awareness we cultivate are all part of the sacred unfolding of life. And when we live with this awareness, with an open heart and mind, we step into the eternal flow of life's purpose. .

CHAPTER 13
MAYA AND THE MIND - THE ILLUSIONS OF THOUGHT, EGO, DESIRE

It was once said that the mind is like a mirror, reflecting whatever it sees, but it's also a mirror that distorts the image. In my early days of exploration, I thought the mind was simply a tool — a thing that processed information, made decisions, and reacted to the world around me. But as I delved deeper into the teachings of yoga and the nature of reality, I began to understand that the mind is not just a passive observer; it is an active creator, constantly shaping and reshaping the world I perceive. And it does so through a lens of illusion.

This illusion — this veil that obscures the truth — is what we call Maya.

The Nature of Maya

Maya is the cosmic illusion that creates the perception of separateness, individuality, and the material world. It is the veil that distorts the reality of our true nature, making us believe that the world of form is all there is. Maya is not a deception in the traditional sense; it is more like a deep fog that clouds the clarity of our perception. It shapes our understanding, causing us to mistake the temporary and ever-changing for the permanent and eternal.

Maya is both external and internal. It exists in the world around us, in the form of our material experiences, relationships, and worldly possessions, but it also resides within us — in the beliefs, patterns, and thought structures that bind us. The teachings of yoga tell us that Maya is the reason why we experience life through a lens of duality. We see ourselves as separate from others, from nature, and from the universe. We identify with our bodies, our thoughts, and our emotions, and through this identification, we create a sense of self that is separate from the whole.

But in reality, we are not separate. We are part of the infinite, ever-present consciousness that is the source of all creation. Maya is the veil that causes us to forget this fundamental truth.

The Role of the Mind

The mind plays a pivotal role in creating and maintaining the illusion of Maya. It is through the mind that we experience the world, and it is through the mind that the illusion of separateness is perpetuated. The mind constructs identities, narratives, and beliefs, and through these mental filters, we experience the world in fragmented pieces. Every thought, every emotion, and every perception is colored by the beliefs we hold, creating a reality that feels real, but is, in essence, a projection of our own mind.

The mind creates layers upon layers of thought, often without our conscious awareness. We are constantly thinking, analyzing, and reacting, rarely pausing to simply be present. We identify with these thoughts and emotions, believing them to be who we are. But when we start to look deeply, we begin to see that these thoughts and emotions are fleeting, transient. They come and go, just like the waves of the ocean. And yet, we often hold onto them, believing that they define us.

In this way, the mind constructs an identity — an ego — that serves as the center of the experience. The ego is the part of the mind that identifies with the body, the thoughts, the emotions, and the desires. It is the sense of "I" — the idea that "I am this body," "I am this thought," or "I am this emotion." This identification with the ego is what keeps us trapped in Maya.

The Ego and the Illusion of Separation

The ego is the root of our illusion of separation. It creates the feeling of individuality, of being distinct from others, from the world, and from the divine. It is through the ego that we experience duality: pleasure and pain, success and failure, love and fear. The ego constantly seeks validation, security, and control, and in doing so, it perpetuates the cycle of attachment and aversion.

This sense of separation is the core of the illusion. The ego convinces us that we are separate from the world and that our happiness depends on the external world — on the things we accumulate, the relationships we form, and the roles we play. But the more we identify with the ego, the more we become bound to the world of form and duality. We believe that our happiness depends on external conditions, and when those conditions change, so too does our sense of happiness.

In truth, however, the ego is an illusion. It is not the real self, but a false identity created by the mind. The real self — the Atman — is beyond the ego, beyond the mind, beyond the body. It is the eternal, unchanging consciousness that is present in every moment, in every being, and in every experience. The more we identify with the ego, the more we become entangled in Maya, the more we forget our true nature.

Desire and the Continuation of the Illusion

Desire is another powerful force that sustains the illusion of Maya. It is the yearning for something outside of ourselves that keeps us trapped in the cycle of attachment and aversion. When we desire something, we project the belief that our happiness or fulfillment depends on it. But as soon as we acquire it, the happiness is fleeting, and the desire shifts to something else. This constant cycle of desire and fulfillment, then disappointment, perpetuates the illusion that our happiness is external — that it depends on something outside of us.

In the yogic view, desire is not inherently bad. It is a natural part of human life. However, when desires are rooted in attachment and identification with the ego, they keep us bound to the illusion of separation. The more we chase external desires, the more we reinforce the idea that we are incomplete and that our happiness is dependent on external circumstances. But true fulfillment comes not from satisfying external desires, but from realizing the truth of who we are — from awakening to our own divine nature.

The Path of Awakening

The path of yoga is a path of awakening from the illusions of the mind, the ego, and desire. It is a journey of moving beyond the identification with the ego and realizing the truth of the self — the Atman — which is one with Brahman, the ultimate reality. This awakening does not happen overnight. It is a gradual process of disidentifying with the mind, the body, and the ego, and coming into direct experience of the self.

Through practices such as meditation, mindfulness, self-inquiry, and the study of sacred teachings, we begin to peel back the layers of illusion. We start to see that the thoughts, emotions, and desires that have shaped our identity are not who we truly are. As we go deeper into the practice, we begin to experience moments of clarity, stillness, and peace. In these moments, the veil of Maya lifts, and we catch a glimpse of the truth that lies beyond the mind.

Ultimately, the goal of yoga is to transcend the illusion of Maya and realize our oneness with the divine. When we do so, we are freed from the cycle of birth and death, the cycle of suffering and desire. We realize that we are not separate from the world, from others, or from the divine. We are that — we are the infinite, ever-present consciousness that pervades all things. And in this realization, we find true freedom and peace.

The mind, the ego, and desire are the key players in the illusion of Maya. They create the sense of separation and individuality, trapping us in a world of duality and desire. But through the path of yoga, we can awaken to the truth of who we are — the eternal, unchanging self. When we stop identifying with the mind and ego, and begin to see through the illusion, we can experience life as it truly is — a unified, interconnected whole.

The journey is not about rejecting the world or the mind but about seeing through the illusions they create. It is about awakening to the truth of our own nature and realizing that we are already whole, already complete. And in that realization, we can experience true peace, true happiness, and true freedom. .

CHAPTER 14
THE GUNAS & NATURE OF REALITY - HOW OUR INNER STATE IS INFLUENCED BY SATTVA, RAJAS, TAMAS

There was a time when I thought life was simply a matter of choices and actions, and that our experiences were just a series of random events. But as I walked deeper into the wisdom of yoga and began to understand the gunas — the three fundamental qualities that govern our mind, body, and spirit — everything began to make sense. The way I thought, acted, and even perceived the world around me was not a random sequence of events. It was deeply influenced by these primal forces, or gunas, that shape every aspect of reality.

The gunas — Sattva, Rajas, and Tamas — are the foundational qualities of nature, the three primary forces that govern the material world and the human experience. In yogic philosophy, the gunas are seen as the forces that shape the mind and the world. They are present in everything — in our thoughts, our emotions, our actions, and even in the way we perceive and interact with the world. Understanding how these three qualities play out in our lives can lead to profound insights into the nature of reality and the path to liberation.

Sattva: The Quality of Purity and Balance

Sattva is the quality of purity, harmony, and balance. It is the essence of clarity, wisdom, and goodness. When sattva predominates in our mind and actions, we feel calm, peaceful, and centered. Our thoughts are clear, our heart is open, and our actions are driven by a sense of truth and compassion. Sattva is the quality of light, and it reflects the higher nature of the soul. It allows us to connect with our true self, with others, and with the universe in a way that is aligned with peace and love.

In a state of sattva, the mind is calm and untroubled. There is an inner stillness that allows us to see the world without distortion, free from the noise of ego and desire. This clarity of mind enables us to act in harmony with our higher purpose, to make decisions based on wisdom rather than impulse or emotion.

When we cultivate sattva in our lives, we move closer to self-realization. It is through sattvic qualities that we experience true joy, contentment, and inner peace. Practices like meditation, yoga, and mindfulness help to increase sattva, allowing us to tap into a deeper state of being, one that is free from the fluctuations of the mind and the distractions of the world.

However, it's important to understand that sattva is not a static state. It is dynamic and always in flux. While sattva brings clarity and peace, it can also create attachment to these states. Even in a state of peace, there is the potential for the ego to arise, to desire that peace, and thus create imbalance. The key is not to become attached to sattva itself, but to let it guide us towards a deeper understanding of our true nature.

Rajas: The Quality of Activity and Desire

Rajas is the quality of activity, motion, and desire. It is the driving force behind our actions, passions, and ambitions. When rajas predominates in our mind and actions, we feel restless, agitated, and driven by desires that are often rooted in ego and attachment. Rajas is the energy of movement, constantly seeking something more — more wealth, more power, more pleasure, more validation.

While rajas is necessary for action and progress in life, when it is out of balance, it leads to stress, anxiety, and a sense of never being satisfied. The constant striving for more creates a cycle of desire that is never fully fulfilled. The restless mind fueled by rajas constantly chases fleeting pleasures and external achievements, only to find that they do not bring lasting peace or contentment.

The challenge with rajas is that it clouds the mind. It creates a sense of identification with the external world, making us believe that our happiness lies in things, in success, in status. We become caught up in the pursuit of desires that are often disconnected from our true self. This sense of disconnection causes us to experience life as chaotic, unpredictable, and unsatisfactory.

However, rajas is also the force that allows us to grow and evolve. It pushes us to act, to create, to strive for something better. It is through rajas that we can find purpose, set goals, and work toward achieving them. But when rajas becomes excessive and uncontrolled, it leads to burnout, dissatisfaction, and a sense of being lost in the noise of life. The key is to channel rajas in a balanced way, allowing it to fuel purposeful action while not being consumed by it.

Tamas: The Quality of Inertia and Ignorance

Tamas is the quality of inertia, ignorance, and darkness. It is the force that causes stagnation, lethargy, and confusion. When tamas predominates in our mind and actions, we feel apathetic, lazy, and uninspired. Tamas is the state of being stuck — stuck in old patterns, stuck in fear, stuck in ignorance. It is the energy that resists change and keeps us locked in cycles of negative thinking, unhealthy habits, and emotional numbness.

Tamas is not inherently bad. Like rajas, it has a purpose. It provides us with the rest and stillness we need to recover and rejuvenate. But when tamas becomes excessive, it leads to inertia, depression, and a lack of motivation. We may become trapped in unhealthy patterns of thinking and behavior, unable to move forward or change. The mind becomes clouded, and we lose touch with our higher self, becoming lost in the darkness of ignorance.

It is important to remember that tamas is not something to fear or reject. It is a natural part of the process of life. In the cycle of creation and destruction, tamas is the energy that allows for rest and dissolution. It is through tamas that we experience deep rest, sleep, and contemplation. However, when tamas dominates, it becomes difficult to see beyond the present moment, and we lose touch with the larger picture of life.

The key is to recognize when tamas has overtaken us and to gently guide ourselves back into balance. Through practices like mindfulness, physical activity, and self-awareness, we can slowly break free from the grip of tamas and begin to move back toward sattva, towards clarity, peace, and understanding.

The Dance of the Gunas: Balancing the Forces

The gunas are not static. They are dynamic forces, constantly shifting and interacting with one another. They are in constant flux, both within us and in the world around us. Every thought, every action, every emotion is influenced by these three qualities. Our inner state is always changing, and the balance of sattva, rajas, and tamas determines how we perceive and experience reality.

Understanding the gunas allows us to cultivate awareness of our inner state and to make conscious choices about how we respond to the world. When we are aware of the influence of rajas, we can choose to bring more stillness and mindfulness into our lives. When we feel the weight of tamas, we can gently move towards action and clarity. And when we are in a state of sattva, we can deepen our connection to our true self, staying grounded in peace and wisdom.

Yoga is the practice that helps us harmonize the gunas. Through regular practice, we can cultivate more sattva, balance the excess of rajas, and lift ourselves out of the stagnation of tamas. It is through this balance that we can transcend the fluctuations of the mind and step into a state of inner peace and clarity.

As I learned to understand the gunas, I began to see them not as obstacles, but as a part of the natural flow of life. Life is a dance of energy — a constant interplay of forces that shape our experience. The key is not to reject one guna or embrace another but to cultivate balance, awareness, and conscious action.

Sattva, rajas, and tamas are all part of the same reality — they are the building blocks of the universe. By understanding them, we can step into a deeper awareness of ourselves and the world around us. Through yoga and self-awareness, we can navigate the dance of the gunas with grace and wisdom, moving towards greater peace, fulfillment, and alignment with our higher self.

PART III
COSMOLOGY, CONSCIOUSNESS & CREATION

CHAPTER 15
THE CREATION OF THE UNIVERSE

The question of the creation of the universe has intrigued both spiritual thinkers and scientists for millennia. Across cultures, various traditions offer unique perspectives on how the cosmos came into being. In the Bhagavad Gita, as well as in the teachings of many yogis, the creation of the universe is not viewed as a singular event with a definitive beginning, but rather as a cyclical process—an eternal flow of creation, preservation, and dissolution. This timeless view of the universe as a dynamic cycle of existence resonates deeply within the realms of both philosophy and spirituality. Let us delve into how the Bhagavad Gita presents the creation of the universe and how this aligns with the profound insights of yogic philosophy.

The Creation According to the Bhagavad Gita

In the Bhagavad Gita, Lord Krishna reveals that the creation of the universe is part of an ongoing and cyclical process. The Gita does not emphasize a linear "beginning" in the conventional sense, but instead offers a vision of the universe as an eternal cycle of creation, preservation, and destruction. This understanding is intricately linked to two core concepts: Brahman (the ultimate reality) and Prakriti (the material energy or nature).

1. The Role of Brahman (The Ultimate Reality)

Krishna explains in the Bhagavad Gita that Brahman, the Supreme Reality, is both the source and the sustainer of the universe. From Brahman, all creation emanates, and everything in the universe is ultimately a manifestation of this formless and eternal essence. Creation, therefore, is not a random event but an unfolding of this divine energy in the material world.

Gita:

"The divine energy of God, which is inherent in nature, is responsible for the creation, preservation, and destruction of the universe."

Krishna further explains that Prakriti (the material energy) operates under the guidance and direction of Ishvara (God or the Supreme Being). Creation unfolds as a manifestation of divine energy through the material world, and this cycle of creation and destruction continues eternally.

2. The Cyclical Nature of Creation

One of the central ideas in the Bhagavad Gita is the concept of time (Kala) as a manifestation of the divine, and the universe's creation occurs within an infinite cycle. Krishna teaches that the universe goes through cycles of creation, existence, and dissolution, which are recurring and eternal. This view of the universe as a never-ending flow aligns with the idea of Yugas—the four great ages, each having distinct qualities and patterns of time.

Gita:

"I am time, the great destroyer of the world, and I have come to consume all people. With the exception of you [the Pandavas], all the soldiers here on both sides will be slain."

In this verse, Krishna identifies Time as an agent of destruction, which is also responsible for both creation and the eventual dissolution of the universe. Everything in the material world is governed by time and must pass through cycles of birth, growth, decay, and death. This continuous flow is the very essence of the cosmic process.

3. Creation Through the Interaction of Purusha and Prakriti

The creation process is also articulated in the Bhagavad Gita as the dynamic interaction between Purusha (the spirit or consciousness) and Prakriti (material nature). Purusha is the active, conscious principle, while Prakriti is the passive, material aspect of reality. The interplay between these two forces gives rise to the material world and all phenomena within it.

Gita:

"The three gunas (modes of nature)—Sattva, Rajas, and Tamas—are the qualities of Prakriti, and it is through their interaction that creation occurs."

Here, Krishna reveals that the three gunas—Sattva (goodness), Rajas (passion), and Tamas (ignorance)—are the forces that govern Prakriti. Their interaction brings about creation, and it is the balance of these forces that determines the nature of the material world and the experiences of the beings within it.

The Three Gunas: Sattva, Rajas, and Tamas

In the Bhagavad Gita, Krishna elaborates on the three gunas as intrinsic qualities of Prakriti (nature) that bind the eternal soul (Atman) to the physical body. These three forces—Sattva, Rajas, and Tamas—shape not only the physical universe but also the psychological and emotional experiences of individuals.

- **Sattva**: Represents purity, knowledge, and harmony. It is associated with clarity, wisdom, and a calm mind.
- **Rajas**: Represents activity, desire, and passion. It is characterized by restlessness, attachment, and an unending pursuit of desires.
- **Tamas**: Represents inertia, ignorance, and darkness. It leads to confusion, laziness, and delusion.

These gunas are not static; they are in constant flux and influence our thoughts, actions, and perceptions. Each of the three gunas governs different aspects of existence, and their relative predominance affects our spiritual growth and understanding.

The Interplay of the Gunas in Shaping Reality

The material world and the experiences of individuals are shaped by the constant interplay of the three gunas. Each guna has a distinct influence on our consciousness and behavior:

- **Sattva** promotes clarity, understanding, and purity. When Sattva predominates, the mind is calm, and there is a sense of peace and wisdom, with a deep connection to the universe.
- **Rajas** drives activity, desire, and ambition. It leads to restlessness, attachment, and binds the soul to the cycle of birth and death through actions fueled by desire and craving.
- **Tamas** causes ignorance, delusion, and inertia. It leads to confusion, laziness, and a lack of awareness, which keep the soul entrenched in the material world and prevents spiritual awakening.

The balance of these three forces shapes our mental state, behavior, and ultimately, our spiritual progress.

Cultivating Sattva for Spiritual Growth

To transcend the binding effects of Rajas and Tamas, spiritual practitioners must focus on cultivating Sattva—the quality of purity and wisdom. This can be achieved through various means:

- ○ **Engaging in selfless actions**: Performing duties without attachment to the results, as taught in Karma Yoga.
- ○ **Practicing meditation and mindfulness**: Developing inner peace, mental clarity, and connection with the divine.
- ○ **Adopting a balanced lifestyle**: Maintaining harmony in thoughts, words, and actions, and fostering an environment conducive to spiritual growth.

By cultivating Sattva, one can transcend the disturbances of Rajas and Tamas, thereby attaining a state of equilibrium that leads to spiritual liberation (moksha).

Scriptural References

The Bhagavad Gita offers deep insights into the nature of the gunas and their influence on our lives:

- ○ "Sattva, Rajas, and Tamas, these three gunas, born of Prakriti, bind the imperishable soul to the body."
- ○ Descriptions of how each guna influences the mind and behavior, and the impact of their predominance.
- ○ Indicators of the predominance of each guna in an individual's nature, and how these influence their actions and spiritual growth.

These verses offer a comprehensive understanding of how the gunas operate within the universe and within each individual. By recognizing and understanding their effects, one can make conscious choices that foster clarity, peace, and ultimate liberation.

The creation of the universe, as described in the Bhagavad Gita, reflects a profound understanding of the cyclical and dynamic nature of existence. Through the interaction of Brahman, Prakriti, and the three gunas, the universe unfolds in an eternal flow of creation, preservation, and dissolution. By understanding the roles of these forces in shaping our reality, and by cultivating the sattvic qualities within ourselves, we can transcend the limitations of the material world, attaining spiritual freedom and liberation from the cycle of birth and death.

In essence, the teachings of the Bhagavad Gita provide a roadmap not only for understanding the creation of the universe but also for navigating the path toward self-realization and ultimate spiritual fulfillment.

CHAPTER 16
THE YOGIC UNDERSTANDING OF THE CREATION OF UNIVERSE

In the vast and profound tradition of yoga, the creation of the universe is often explored through the lens of a cosmic process of manifestation and dissolution. Yogic philosophies present the universe as a dynamic interplay between consciousness (Purusha) and material nature (Prakriti). This understanding provides a deep insight into the cyclical nature of existence, where the universe continuously evolves, dissolves, and re-manifests in an eternal rhythm.

1. The Cosmic Process and the Role of Purusha

Within many yogic philosophies, particularly those within the Samkhya and Advaita Vedanta traditions, the creation of the universe is understood as the outcome of the interaction between Purusha (the eternal consciousness) and Prakriti (the material energy). This union of consciousness and matter is the foundation of all creation, with each cycle of manifestation being a spontaneous unfolding of the infinite consciousness into the finite material realm.

In this view, creation is not a singular event but rather a continuous cycle, driven by the interplay between these two essential forces. The universe is seen as an expression of Purusha, manifesting through Prakriti, where matter is imbued with the essence of consciousness. This dynamic relationship results in the cosmic order, unfolding in phases of creation, preservation, and dissolution.

Example from the Yoga Sutras of Patanjali:
Patanjali, in his renowned Yoga Sutras, articulates the process of manifestation (Srishti) and dissolution (Pralaya) within the context of the

eternal cycle of the gunas—the three qualities of nature (Sattva, Rajas, and Tamas). Creation occurs when the gunas interact and come into balance, leading to the manifestation of the material world. When the gunas return to their unmanifest state, the universe dissolves back into its pure, formless potential, awaiting the next cycle of manifestation.

2. The Role of Divine Energy: Shakti

In many Tantric and yogic traditions, creation is understood as a dynamic, unfolding expression of Shakti, the divine feminine energy. Shakti is believed to be the creative power of the universe that emanates from the Supreme Being. In this framework, Shakti is not merely a passive force, but an active, creative energy that underpins the very fabric of existence.

Just as the Bhagavad Gita speaks of Prakriti as the material energy under the direction of the Supreme Being, many yogic systems associate this creative energy with Shakti, which is the active and dynamic force of creation. The universe is seen as Shakti's divine manifestation, constantly evolving through the interaction between consciousness (Purusha) and energy (Shakti).

Example from Yogic Philosophy:
In Tantric traditions, the creation of the universe is viewed as the divine union between Shiva (the supreme consciousness) and Shakti (the cosmic energy). This union is the source of all creation, and the continuous interplay between Shiva and Shakti propels the world through cycles of creation, preservation, and destruction. The universe, thus, is an ongoing manifestation of the Divine Feminine energy, eternally creative and ever-evolving.

3. The Concept of Cosmic Cycles: Kalachakra and Yugas

Much like the Bhagavad Gita's description of a cyclical creation, yogic philosophies embrace the idea of Kalachakra—the wheel of time—that governs the universe. These cycles of time are represented by the Yugas—the four great ages—each marked by different qualities and stages of existence. The universe moves through these stages of creation, sustenance, and dissolution, and each Yuga brings with it a different aspect of reality and cosmic rhythm.

In this model, creation and dissolution are not linear but unfold according to these cosmic cycles, with each cycle representing a complete journey of manifestation and return to the source. The process is governed by the dynamic interplay of Purusha and Prakriti, as well as the eternal rhythm of the gunas.

Example from the Yoga of the Divine:

In the teachings of the Upanishads and the philosophy of Sri Aurobindo, creation is seen as the unfolding of divine consciousness into material form. This descent of consciousness into matter is the process of manifestation, followed by a return to pure consciousness in dissolution. The ultimate goal is to realize the inherent unity of Purusha (spirit) and Prakriti (matter), which leads to spiritual liberation (moksha). By transcending the illusions of the material world, one merges back into the infinite consciousness from which the universe has emerged.

The Yogic Vision of Creation

The Bhagavad Gita offers a profound understanding of creation as cyclical, governed by Brahman (the Supreme Reality) and Prakriti (material nature). The unfolding of the universe follows the eternal dance of creation, preservation, and dissolution, with time (Kala) playing a central role in each phase. Everything in the universe, as described in the Gita, is ultimately a manifestation of God's energy.

In yogic traditions, creation is understood as the unfolding of consciousness into the material world. In Samkhya and Advaita Vedanta, the universe is the result of the interaction between Purusha (spirit) and Prakriti (matter). In Tantric traditions, creation is seen as the dynamic energy of Shakti, manifesting through the eternal union of Shiva and Shakti. This view emphasizes the divine energy that perpetually drives creation, bringing forth new cycles of existence and dissolution in a timeless flow.

Thus, in both the Bhagavad Gita and various yogic philosophies, creation is portrayed as a dynamic, cyclical process—a manifestation of the eternal interplay between consciousness and material nature. It is an unfolding mystery that invites us to reflect upon the nature of reality and our place within it, ultimately guiding us toward the realization of the unity between the divine spirit and the material world.

Here is How the Yogis Explain the Creation of Universe in a Simple Way

"In the beginning, there was only Silence—still, unbroken, and infinite.

Then, from the void, the first tremor stirred, a soundless pulse rippling through the nothingness.

This vibration, a wave of divine energy, shattered the stillness and brought forth the first breath of creation.

It was the Sound of Shiva, a primal roar, deep and infinite, echoing through the fabric of existence.

As the sound expanded, it danced through the cosmos, weaving threads of energy that vibrated with infinite potential.

And within these vibrations, forms began to emerge, swirling from the primordial ether like sparks from a divine fire.

Each vibration carried a pattern, a blueprint of life and matter, shaping the vastness of the universe.

This sound, the very essence of creation, became the essence of Shiva himself.

Rudra's cry, fierce and untamed, reverberated through the void, not in anger, but in the pulse of the cosmos unfolding.

It was not a cry of destruction but a declaration of the eternal cycle, a reminder that in every ending lies a new beginning.

From the first note of that sound, countless vibrations emerged, some deep and thunderous, others light and fleeting.

They blended together, creating a symphony of existence, a cosmic song whose melodies formed the foundations of all that is.

From each vibration arose a shape, a form—a being, an atom, a galaxy, all spinning in harmony with the divine rhythm.

Creation itself was born from this eternal sound, vibrating with the cosmic pulse.

The connection between Sound and Form was inseparable, each vibration crafting a world, each note of Shiva's music sculpting the universe.

The harmony of the cosmos is this sacred union, this unending flow of energy that continues to reverberate through space and time,

forever intertwining the unseen with the seen, the formless with the formed."

Key Elements in the Enhanced Imagery:

Silence as the Beginning:

The passage begins with Silence as the origin, emphasizing a state of unmanifested potential, a key aspect of Shiva's essence. In the Vedic worldview, Silence (or Shunyata) is considered the primal state before creation.

Primal Vibration:

The sound that emerges is described as a "tremor", a "pulse", emphasizing that vibration is not sudden but a slow, cosmic expansion of energy. The imagery of Shiva's primal roar makes this vibration feel immense, ancient, and powerful, symbolizing the birth of time and space.

The Sound of Shiva:

Shiva's sound is likened to a roar, creating the sense that his voice is not just sound but the very force that initiates creation. By calling it a "primal roar", it suggests that Shiva's energy is raw, untamed, and full of creative potential.

Vibrations Creating Form:

The idea that vibrations give rise to forms is emphasized. The forms are not just random but patterns carried within each vibration, highlighting the connection between the formless and the manifest. The imagery of sparks from a divine fire or swirling forms emerging from the ether adds a mystical, visual element to the process of creation.

Cosmic Symphony:

Instead of just listing various vibrations, this version describes them as a "symphony"—a musical, harmonious force. This creates the image of the universe as a living, breathing organism, with each vibration and form playing its part in the greater cosmic order.

Shiva's Role as the Cosmic Conductor:

Shiva is portrayed as the one who plays the symphony—his energy is the driving force behind the vibrations and the forms they create. The passage also suggests that the sound of Shiva continues to reverberate, keeping the universe in motion. This adds a dynamic, ongoing aspect to creation, suggesting that the sound is not a one-time event but an eternal process.

Harmonizing the Seen and Unseen:

The final lines suggest a cosmic harmony, where the seen (the physical world) and the unseen (the spiritual realm) are always in a dance of unity. The vibration (or sound) is what unites them, making creation a never-ending flow of energy, knowledge, and matter.

Why This Imagery Works:

- **Evocative Descriptions:** The enhanced imagery taps into multiple senses—sight, sound, and feeling. It creates a world where vibration and sound are not just abstract concepts but living forces that shape everything around us.
- **Cosmic Drama:** By describing creation as a "cosmic symphony" or "divine song", the passage elevates the process of creation into a grand, cosmic event, which resonates with the idea of the universe as a divine play (Lila) in Hindu thought.
- **Shiva as the Creator:** Shiva is shown as not only the first yogi but also the cosmic force that brings everything into being, highlighting his role as the source of both the manifest and the unmanifest.
- **Non-Duality:** This imagery reinforces the non-dual nature of Shiva, where the formless and formed are seen as two aspects of the same reality, ever intertwined through sound and vibration.

The idea of creation through sound and vibration is a key theme in many Eastern philosophies, especially within Hinduism and Buddhism. By enriching the imagery in this way, we bring the abstract ideas of creation to life, making them more tangible and easier to connect with on a deeper, emotional level. It transforms the concepts of sound, vibration, and form into something not just to be understood intellectually, but felt and experienced in the imagination.

CHAPTER 17
THE JOURNEY OF CONSCIOUSNESS INTO MATTER - A COSMIC PROCESS

The journey of consciousness into matter is a profound and transformative concept found at the heart of many spiritual and philosophical traditions, including the yogic sciences. This process illuminates how pure consciousness (or spirit) descends into the material world, ultimately taking form as the physical universe. In yogic and Vedic philosophy, this journey is intricately linked to the creation of the cosmos, the evolution of life, and the unfolding of the laws governing the universe.

1. Pure Consciousness – The Source of All

At the very beginning of creation, there exists pure consciousness, often referred to as Brahman in Vedic philosophy or Turiya in yogic teachings. This state of consciousness is infinite, formless, and beyond all duality. It is the essence of existence—a vast and undifferentiated awareness where time, space, and matter do not yet exist. This is often described as the unmanifest, the primordial state from which all things arise.

Vedic Concept of Creation:
In the Rig Veda, the universe emanates from Brahman, the source of all potential. Brahman is both immanent (within all things) and transcendent (beyond all things). From this pure, undifferentiated consciousness arises the first impulse of creation, a shift from formlessness to form.

2. The Evolution of Consciousness – The Manifestation of Creation

The descent of consciousness into the material world is a gradual unfolding. In this stage, consciousness begins to differentiate into distinct forces and energies, eventually giving rise to the creation of the universe. This marks the first step from the unmanifest to the manifest.

Prakriti and Purusha:

In yogic philosophy, creation is understood as a cosmic dance between Prakriti (the primal, material nature) and Purusha (the eternal, unchanging consciousness or soul). Prakriti, in its pure and formless state, holds the potential for all creation. The union of Purusha and Prakriti catalyzes the process of manifestation. This interaction is the first spark in the transformation of pure consciousness into the material world.

The Gunas:

The three gunas (qualities or forces of Prakriti)—Sattva (balance, harmony), Rajas (activity, desire), and Tamas (inertia, darkness)—begin to shape the material world. These fundamental qualities interact to create the diversity of forms, behaviors, and experiences that define the universe. Each guna influences the manifestation of reality, contributing to the creation of varied life forms and experiences.

3. The Creation of the Elements

As consciousness continues its journey into matter, it gives rise to the five elements (Pancha Mahabhutas) that form the foundation of the physical universe. These elements are the building blocks of all matter, shaping not only the material world but also the laws that govern it.

- **Ether (Akasha)**: The element of space and sound, providing the medium through which all other elements exist.

- **Air (Vayu)**: The element of movement, wind, and energy.
- **Fire (Agni)**: The element of transformation, heat, and light.
- **Water (Jala)**: The element of fluidity, emotion, and adaptability.
- **Earth (Prithvi)**: The element of solidity, structure, and stability.

These elements come together and interact, giving rise to the physical forms of matter in the universe and shaping the laws of nature that govern existence.

4. The Descent of Consciousness into Life Forms

Once the five elements are formed, they combine to give rise to life. In this stage, the life force (Prana) and consciousness begin to inhabit material forms. The interaction between Purusha (consciousness) and Prakriti (nature) results in the emergence of individual life forms capable of experiencing the world through physical senses.

The Evolution of Life:

As consciousness continues its descent into the material realm, it becomes more individualized. The earliest forms of life are rudimentary, yet over time, through the process of evolution, more complex life forms emerge. While the body may change and evolve, consciousness remains the underlying essence of all beings, though it is often obscured by the physical form.

The Individual Soul (Jiva):

In each living being, the pure consciousness or Atman takes on a limited, individualized form. This Jiva (individual soul) temporarily associates with the body and mind and undergoes the cycles of birth, death, and rebirth (samsara), accumulating experiences and karma throughout its journey.

5. The Duality of Consciousness and Matter

At this stage of existence, there emerges a duality: the eternal, unchanging consciousness (the Self) and the material world. The soul (Atman) becomes entangled with the material body and mind, and the journey through the physical world continues.

The Veil of Maya:

The material world is often described as a veil of Maya, an illusion that obscures the true nature of consciousness. Through Maya, beings mistakenly identify themselves with the physical body and mind, forgetting their spiritual essence. This illusion perpetuates the cycle of suffering and confusion.

Ignorance (Avidya):

The journey of consciousness into matter is marked by Avidya—ignorance, the mistaken belief that the self is defined by the physical body and mind, and that matter is the ultimate reality. This ignorance binds the soul to the endless cycle of birth and rebirth, keeping it unaware of its true nature and connection to the Divine.

6. The Path of Awakening: Realizing the Oneness of Consciousness and Matter

The ultimate goal of this cosmic journey is the realization of the oneness of consciousness and matter. Through this realization, the individual soul comes to understand that its true essence is not separate from the universal consciousness.

Spiritual Practices:

Through practices like meditation, self-inquiry, yoga, and detachment, one can pierce the illusion of Maya and rediscover the true, formless nature of consciousness. When a person recognizes that their essence is one with the universal consciousness, they achieve self-realization and transcend the cycle of suffering and rebirth.

7. Returning to the Source: The Final Unity

Once the soul has realized its true nature, it returns to its source—pure consciousness. The individual self merges back into the universal consciousness, and the duality between consciousness and matter is transcended. This state is known as Kaivalya (liberation) or Moksha (freedom), where the soul is liberated from the limitations of the material world and experiences ultimate unity with the Divine.

- **Pure Consciousness (Brahman)**: The unmanifest, infinite source of all that exists.

- **Prakriti (Material Nature)**: The first differentiation, leading to the manifestation of the universe.

- **The Five Elements**: The foundation of the physical world and its inherent properties.

- **Individual Souls (Jivas)**: Consciousness enters individualized forms, becoming limited by the body and mind.

- **Duality of Consciousness and Matter**: The illusion of separation between the material and spiritual worlds.

- **Spiritual Awakening**: The soul's journey back to its true essence, transcending the illusion of material existence.

- **Union with the Divine**: The soul returns to the original state of unity with pure consciousness.

In essence, the journey of consciousness into matter represents the cosmic process of creation, evolution, and eventual return to the source. It is a cyclical process that reflects the soul's movement through the material world, ultimately seeking the realization of its true nature and its oneness with the universe. This journey is both universal and personal, inviting each soul to transcend the illusion of separation and to awaken to its infinite, divine essence.

CHAPTER 18
THE YOGIC SCIENCE BEHIND YUGAS

The concept of the Yugas offers a profound lens through which we can understand the cyclical nature of time, human evolution, and the shifts in collective consciousness. Rooted in Yogic and Vedic traditions, the Yugas are not simply historical epochs or mythological constructs. They represent energetic and spiritual phases that reflect the ever-changing nature of human awareness. These cycles of time are intimately connected to the rise and fall of human consciousness, much like the rhythms of the breath or the changing of seasons.

In this exploration, we will delve deeply into the Yugas, not just as time periods, but as profound spiritual states — both universal and personal — that influence our journey of growth and self-realization.

What Are Yugas?

The term Yuga translates to "age" or "epoch" and represents an era in the vast cycle of cosmic time. The Yogic and Vedic understanding of time is not linear, as seen in conventional history. Instead, it is cyclical — an endless flow, much like the in-breath and out-breath of the universe, or the ever-turning wheel of seasons. Each cycle of time, known as a Yuga, represents a distinct phase in the unfolding of human consciousness and the balance of dharma (righteousness).

The Yugas, in this context, are not just external phases of history but are reflections of the spiritual energy shaping both the individual and the collective human experience. As consciousness ebbs and flows through these periods, humanity experiences growth, decline, and eventual renewal.

The Four Yugas: Duration, Meaning, and Consciousness Levels

The four Yugas — Satya Yuga, Treta Yuga, Dvapara Yuga, and Kali Yuga — represent the evolution of both the human spirit and the cosmic energy. Each Yuga is characterized by a distinct level of dharma, and each reflects a particular phase in the development of human consciousness. .

Yuga	Duration (Traditional View)	Dharma (Righteousness)	Human Consciousness
Satya Yuga (*Golden Age*)	~1.7 million years	100%	Pure, spiritual, peaceful
Treta Yuga (*Silver Age*)	~1.3 million years	75%	Some ego, rituals begin
Dvapara Yuga (*Bronze Age*)	~860,000 years	50%	Duality, more material focus
Kali Yuga (*Iron Age*)	~432,000 years	25%	Confusion, conflict, materialism

In these cycles, the consciousness of humanity rises and falls, with Satya Yuga marking the height of spiritual purity and Kali Yuga reflecting a state of confusion, ignorance, and materialism.

Yogic Interpretation of the Yugas

From a Yogic perspective, the Yugas represent not only chronological eras but the ascent and descent of spiritual awareness over time. Each Yuga embodies a distinct phase in the evolution of consciousness, where humanity either aligns with or diverges from its true nature.

Satya Yuga represents the Golden Age, where humans naturally live in harmony with the divine and effortlessly access higher spiritual states. Yogis in this era experience profound meditative states, unlocking siddhis (inner powers) and connecting with higher dimensions of existence. The human consciousness is pure, and the connection to the universal truth is unbroken.

In Kali Yuga, by contrast, the material world and the ego dominate. The subtle realms fade, and spiritual awareness becomes clouded by illusion (Maya), making it increasingly difficult to recognize the deeper truths of existence. Despite the darkness of this age, it is also an era of immense opportunity — for even the smallest spiritual efforts can lead to profound transformation.

Yugas and the Human System: Microcosm = Macrocosm

In Yogic teachings, the phrase "What is in the cosmos is also within you" beautifully encapsulates the idea that the cycles of the Yugas are not external events but internal realities. Each individual is both a microcosm of the greater macrocosm. The Yugas, therefore, are not just cosmic phases; they are energetic states of consciousness that we experience within ourselves.

If your mind is at peace, aligned with truth, and open to higher awareness, you are living in a state akin to Satya Yuga.

If you are ruled by ego, fear, and attachment to material desires, you are experiencing a more Kali Yuga state, regardless of the external time period.

The key message from yogis is simple yet profound: "Don't worry about the Yuga outside. Transform the Yuga within." The power to shift from Kali Yuga to Satya Yuga lies within each of us, in the choices we make, the practices we embrace, and the spiritual path we walk.

How Yogis Navigated the Yugas

Throughout the Yugas, spiritual practices have evolved to align with the changing energetic conditions. Each Yuga demands different approaches to spiritual growth and connection with the divine:

In Satya Yuga, spiritual practices were direct and pure. Meditation was effortless, and individuals could realize Truth without the need for religious rituals or external guidance. The inner wisdom was self-evident, and human beings lived in perfect harmony with the divine order.

In Treta Yuga, as consciousness began to contract, rituals and yajnas (fire ceremonies) became essential for maintaining a connection with the divine. Kings and sages upheld dharma, guiding society through spiritual teachings. The ego began to emerge, and people started to rely on rituals to support their spiritual progress.

In Dvapara Yuga, duality became pronounced. Humans introduced scriptures, temples, and idols to focus worship. This era witnessed the rise of conflict and ego, as the material world began to dominate. The practice of rituals became increasingly formalized, and the gap between the individual soul and the divine began to widen.

In Kali Yuga, with the ego at its peak, dharma is at its lowest. Spirituality in this age requires dedicated effort and discipline. The inner work of yoga, mantra, and meditation becomes the primary means of transcending the illusions of the world. Although spiritual progress is more challenging, it is also the age in which great spiritual advancements can be made — if one dares to look inward.

Yugas as a Cycle: Yogic Cosmology

The Yugas are not linear but cyclical, like the turning of a wheel or the changing of the seasons. This cyclical nature is mirrored in the broader cosmic dance of the universe. According to Yogic cosmology, the Yugas are intricately connected to the position of our solar system in the galaxy.

As the solar system moves closer to the galactic center — the spiritual sun — consciousness rises, and the world experiences an age of higher awareness (Satya Yuga). Conversely, as the solar system moves away from the galactic center, consciousness falls, leading to darker periods like Kali Yuga.

Sri Yukteswar, the guru of Paramahansa Yogananda, famously taught that we are transitioning from Kali Yuga to Dvapara Yuga. This period marks the awakening of subtle knowledge and spiritual energy, signaling a shift in human consciousness toward a new era of enlightenment.

What Yogic Science Teaches About Kali Yuga

While Kali Yuga is often characterized as an age of confusion, materialism, and spiritual decline, it is also a time of immense opportunity for transformation. This era is one in which the inner light shines brightest, if one dares to turn inward and engage in deep spiritual practice.

In Kali Yuga, the ego can be loud and overpowering, but even a small amount of sadhana (spiritual effort) can lead to great results. Practices such as:

- Mantra Yoga (the power of sacred sound)
- Kriya Yoga (breathing techniques for energy control)
- Bhakti Yoga (devotion to the divine)
- Inner engineering (transforming the mind and consciousness)

These practices are more crucial than ever in Kali Yuga, offering a direct path to spiritual freedom and self-realization.

As one yogic adage says, "In Kali Yuga, the darkest of ages, the light within shines the brightest — if one dares to look inward."

The Eternal Cycles of Consciousness

The science of the Yugas teaches us that time is not a linear progression but a series of cyclical stages that govern both the cosmos and the human experience. By understanding these cycles, we gain insight into the rhythms of our own consciousness. Even in the darkest ages — like Kali Yuga — there is always the possibility of transformation, of returning to the truth and light within.

Ultimately, the Yugas remind us that spiritual growth is not bound by external conditions but is a matter of internal awakening. Whether we find ourselves in Kali Yuga or Satya Yuga, the choice remains the same: to turn inward and realize the eternal truth that lies within us all.

CHAPTER 19
THE 36 TATTVAS - THE DECENT OF CONSCIOUSNESS INTO MATTER

The 36 Tattvas are a central philosophical concept within Shaiva Siddhanta, Kashmir Shaivism, and other non-dual Tantric and Yogic systems. These Tattvas (from the Sanskrit word tattva, meaning "thatness" or "principles of reality") explain the process by which pure consciousness (Shiva) manifests as the material universe, unfolding in layers from the most subtle and formless realms to the tangible, physical world we experience.

In this intricate system, the Tattvas reveal the evolution of consciousness from its original, pure state to the realm of matter. As such, they provide a framework for understanding the journey of the individual soul (Jiva) and the process of creation. The Tattvas also offer insight into the path of spiritual liberation, where a practitioner can reverse this descent of consciousness—ascending from the material to the divine, from matter back to Shiva.

The Tattvas are grouped into distinct categories, each representing a different level of reality. These categories range from the most pure and unmanifested aspects of consciousness to the most material and gross forms of existence.

The 36 Tattvas: The Descent of Consciousness into Matter

The 36 Tattvas are divided into five broad categories, progressing from the highest spiritual principles to the most material aspects of creation. These categories reflect the journey of consciousness as it moves from the formless and unified state of Shiva to the fragmented and dualistic nature of the world we perceive through our senses.

Śuddha Tattvas (Pure Tattvas) – Tattvas 1 to 5
Śuddhāśuddha Tattvas (Pure–Impure Tattvas) – Tattvas 6 to 11
Ātma Tattvas (Soul-Level Tattvas) – Tattvas 12 to 16
Indriya Tattvas (Senses & Organs) – Tattvas 17 to 27
Bhūta Tattvas (The Gross Elements) – Tattvas 28 to 36

I. Śuddha Tattvas (Pure Tattvas) – Tattvas 1 to 5

The Śuddha Tattvas represent the realm of absolute purity and unmanifested consciousness. These Tattvas are beyond duality and limitation, existing in the purest state of unity and formlessness. At this level, there is no distinction between subject and object, only undivided consciousness. These Tattvas are not limited by time, space, or form.

- **Śiva** – The highest, undivided consciousness, formless and infinite. It is the absolute, the very foundation of existence.
- **Śakti** – The dynamic creative power of Shiva. It is the will to manifest, the creative force that moves Shiva into expression.
- **Sadāśiva** – The awareness of oneness, where the consciousness begins to move gently toward creation. It is the first stirring of differentiation in pure consciousness.
- **Īśvara** – The moment when consciousness recognizes itself within creation. It sees the divine reflected in the universe and acknowledges its existence in all things.
- **Śuddhavidyā** – The balanced awareness where self and other begin to emerge as distinct but still unified. This is the first hint of differentiation, but there is still harmony.

These five Tattvas are pure and non-dual, existing beyond any forms of limitation or fragmentation.

II. Śuddhāśuddha Tattvas (Pure-Impure Tattvas) – Tattvas 6 to 11

At this stage, limitation and duality begin to manifest. The soul (Jiva) arises here as a limited entity, influenced by various forces that create separation. This category marks the beginning of individuality, where the unmanifest consciousness starts to differentiate and become entangled in the play of duality.

- **Māyā** – The veil of illusion that creates the perception of separation and duality. It is the force that clouds the true nature of reality and causes the soul to forget its oneness with the divine.
- **Kāla** – Time, which limits the soul to the experience of past, present, and future. Time creates the illusion of change and perpetuates the cycle of birth, death, and rebirth.
- **Niyati** – The principle of order and cause-effect. It imposes limitations on the spontaneity of the soul, binding it to the laws of karma and fate.
- **Rāga** – Desire or attachment, which creates craving and aversion. The soul begins to long for experience, pleasure, and fulfillment, creating the cycle of attachment and suffering.
- **Vidyā** – Limited knowledge or the fragmented understanding of reality. The soul perceives the world through the veil of duality, seeing partial truths rather than the whole.
- **Kalā** – Limited ability to act, the finite expression of Shakti. The soul's power is restricted, as opposed to the boundless, infinite power of Shiva.

These six Tattvas give rise to the Jiva (individual soul), which is now limited in its action, perception, and understanding.

III. Ātma Tattvas (Soul-Level Tattvas) – Tattvas 12 to 16

The Ātma Tattvas represent the formation of the subtle body, which encompasses the mind, intellect, ego, and the essence of individuality. These Tattvas correspond to the soul's evolution as it becomes aware of its individuality and its capacity for self-awareness and self-identification.

- **Purusha** – The individual self, the soul that is bound but still conscious of its separation from the divine. It represents the essence of the Jiva.
- **Prakriti** – Primordial matter, the material nature from which the physical universe is made. It is the latent potential for creation.
- **Buddhi** – The higher intellect, the discriminative mind that enables the soul to discern truth from illusion.
- **Ahamkara** – The ego, the sense of "I-ness" or personal identity. It is the force that creates the feeling of separation from the absolute.
- **Manas** – The lower mind, which processes sensory input and gives rise to thoughts, emotions, and perceptions.

These Tattvas constitute the subtle body: the mind, intellect, ego, and the deeper aspects of the individual's inner experience.

IV. Indriya Tattvas (Senses & Organs) – Tattvas 17 to 27

The Indriya Tattvas describe the organs of perception and action. These Tattvas represent how the Jiva engages with the external world, experiencing it through the senses and interacting with it through actions.

Five Jñānendriyas (Sense organs):
- **Śrotra** – Hearing
- **Tvak** – Touch
- **Cakṣus** – Sight

- ○ **Jihvā** – Taste
- ○ **Ghrāṇa** – Smell

Five Karmendriyas (Organs of action):
- ○ **Vāk** – Speech
- ○ **Pāṇi** – Hands
- ○ **Pāda** – Feet
- ○ **Pāyu** – Anus (excretion)
- ○ **Upastha** – Genitals (reproduction)

One Internal Organ:
- ○ **Antaḥkaraṇa** – The combination of intellect, ego, and mind, which processes and interprets the input from the senses.

These Tattvas define how we perceive and act in the world. They form the interface between the individual and the external universe.

V. Bhūta Tattvas (The Gross Elements) – Tattvas 28 to 36

The Bhūta Tattvas represent the gross elements that make up the material universe, including the physical body, nature, and objects. These Tattvas form the foundation of the physical world in which we live.

Five Tanmātras (Subtle elements):
- ○ **Śabda** – Sound
- ○ **Sparśa** – Touch
- ○ **Rūpa** – Form
- ○ **Rasa** – Taste
- ○ **Gandha** – Smell

Five Mahābhūtas (Gross elements):
- ○ **Ākāśa** – Ether (space)
- ○ **Vāyu** – Air

- ◦ **Agni (Tejas)** – Fire
- ◦ **Apas** – Water
- ◦ **Pṛthvī** – Earth

These Tattvas form the physical universe, from the subtle elements that give rise to perception to the gross elements that manifest as matter and form.

Group	Range	Description
Pure (Śuddha)	1–5	Levels of divine consciousness
Mixed (Śuddhāśuddha)	6–11	Limiting principles that create the soul
Soul & Mind (Ātma)	12–16	Individual self, intellect, ego, mind
Senses (Indriyas)	17–27	Organs of perception and action
Matter (Bhūtas)	28–36	Subtle & gross elements (nature & body)

Why This Matters in Yoga & Mysticism

The teachings of the 36 Tattvas are not simply abstract philosophical concepts but powerful tools for spiritual practice and liberation:

Liberation (Moksha): Understanding the process by which pure consciousness descends into matter allows the yogi to reverse the journey—ascending from the gross (material) back to the subtle and ultimately to the pure divine consciousness of Shiva. This process leads to liberation from the limitations of the material world.

Spiritual Practice: Different forms of Yoga—such as Jnana Yoga, Raja Yoga, and Tantra—use these Tattvas to understand the workings of the body, mind, and ego, and ultimately transcend them. By contemplating and meditating on each Tattva, a practitioner can dissolve the limitations and return to their divine essence.

Temple Science & Chakras: The Tattvas are often mirrored in temple architecture and the chakra systems of the body. Each layer of the temple or the energy body corresponds to different Tattvas, with the physical structure reflecting the subtle body's ascent to the divine.

Through understanding the 36 Tattvas, we learn that the journey from pure consciousness to the physical world is not linear but a complex, layered process that can be reversed for spiritual awakening and liberation. By contemplating and embodying these Tattvas, we move closer to the ultimate truth: that we are Shiva, the boundless, eternal consciousness, expressing itself through the material world and ultimately transcending it.

CHAPTER 20
THE 5 KOSHAS - UNVEILING THE LAYERS OF CONSCIOUSNESS

In the ancient yogic sciences, few frameworks offer as profound and holistic an understanding of the human experience as the Pancha Kosha doctrine. Pancha means "five," and Kosha translates to "sheath" or "covering." According to this teaching, a human being is not merely a physical entity — but a multilayered being comprised of five concentric layers, each more subtle than the one before.

These five Koshas represent not only dimensions of our existence but also a spiritual roadmap. The path of yoga and inner inquiry is fundamentally a journey through these layers — from the outermost covering of the physical body to the innermost core, where pure consciousness and bliss reside.

Understanding and working with the Koshas helps us move beyond identification with the body and mind, toward an awakened awareness of the Atman — the eternal Self that exists beyond all layers.

The Five Koshas: An Overview

Kosha	Meaning	Layer	Aspect of Being	Energy Type
Annamaya	Food Body	Physical Body	Flesh, bones, organs	Gross physical matter
Pranamaya	Energy Body	Life Force	Breath, prana, energy flow	Subtle energy
Manomaya	Mind Body	Mental/ Emotional	Thoughts, emotions, memory	Mental/emotio nal energy

Vijnanamaya	Wisdom Body	Intellect/ Insight	Discrimination, intuition	Intellectual energy
Anandamaya	Bliss Body	Pure Being	Stillness, joy, soul essence	Causal/subtlest energy

Each Kosha is interrelated. When one layer is disturbed, the others often follow. Likewise, when we heal and harmonize a deeper layer, we experience profound shifts across all dimensions of our being.

Annamaya Kosha – The Physical Body (Food Sheath)

"Anna" in Sanskrit means food — and this sheath is composed of the food we eat, the air we breathe, and the physical matter that makes up the body. It is the most tangible layer — the body of skin, muscle, bones, and organs that we experience through our five senses.

This is the layer most people identify with exclusively, yet in yogic understanding, it is the outermost shell. Health, flexibility, posture, and physical strength are expressions of the vitality of this kosha.

Practices that support Annamaya Kosha:
- Hatha Yoga (Asanas)
- Clean, sattvic (pure) diet
- Fasting or detox rituals
- Walking barefoot on natural earth (earthing)

When this Kosha is healthy, we feel grounded, nourished, and vibrant. But when imbalanced, we experience physical fatigue, illness, and disconnection from our body's intelligence.

Pranamaya Kosha – The Energy Body (Vital Sheath)

This sheath is composed of Prana, the vital life force that animates the body. While it is often associated with the breath, Prana is far more than air — it is the subtle energy that flows through 72,000 nadis (energy channels), energizing every cell and organ.

Just as the body has a bloodstream, the energy body has a pranic flow. When this flow is disrupted, physical and emotional disturbances follow. Pranamaya Kosha acts as a bridge between the physical body and the mental-emotional body.

Practices that nourish Pranamaya Kosha:

- Pranayama (breath control techniques)
- Kriya Yoga
- Surya Kriya or Surya Namaskar
- Breath-focused meditations

A balanced Pranamaya Kosha results in vitality, mental clarity, and emotional stability. It is the subtle electricity that keeps the system alive and responsive.

Manomaya Kosha – The Mental Body (Mind Sheath)

"Manas" means mind, and this sheath encompasses our mental patterns, emotional reactions, and sensory processing. It is constantly active, interpreting the world based on conditioning, past experiences, and emotional memory.

This Kosha determines our habitual reactions — our likes and dislikes, fears and desires. It is also the layer most affected by external stimuli, making it unstable and prone to fluctuations unless guided by deeper awareness.

Practices to balance Manomaya Kosha:

- Chanting and mantra repetition (Japa)
- Mindfulness and conscious observation
- Sensory withdrawal (Pratyahara)
- Rituals that invoke sacredness

When this Kosha is calm and clear, the mind becomes a tool for presence and devotion, rather than a source of anxiety or distraction.

Vijnanamaya Kosha – The Wisdom Body (Discriminative Sheath)

"Vijnana" means higher knowledge, and this sheath relates to the buddhi — the faculty of discernment, insight, and spiritual wisdom. It enables us to differentiate between truth and illusion, ego and soul, reaction and response.

This Kosha governs moral clarity, intuition, and inner direction. It is the gateway to wisdom — not intellectual knowledge, but the deep knowing that arises from inner silence and awareness.

Practices to awaken Vijnanamaya Kosha:

- Self-inquiry (e.g., "Who am I?")
- Study of sacred texts (Svadhyaya)
- Contemplative silence
- Meditation on universal truths

As this Kosha unfolds, we begin to live with greater authenticity, making choices that align with the soul rather than the ego. It is where spiritual maturity begins to emerge.

Anandamaya Kosha – The Bliss Body (Causal Sheath)

"Ananda" means bliss, and this final sheath is the most subtle, the closest to the core of who we are. It is not bliss in the sense of fleeting pleasure, but a deep, unshakable stillness, a quiet joy that is untouched by external circumstances.

This is the threshold to the Self (Atman). It cannot be reached by effort, only by dissolution. You do not "do" something to experience Anandamaya Kosha — you surrender into it.

Practices to enter Anandamaya Kosha:

- Deep, silent meditation
- Bhakti Yoga (devotion)
- Samadhi (absorption)
- States of unconditional love and surrender

Experiencing this sheath is experiencing oneness with existence — a sense of being that is free, whole, and eternal.

The Yogic Journey Through the Koshas

The process of yoga is fundamentally an inward journey through these five layers:

Kosha	Experience	Goal/Result
Annamaya	Physical body	Health, grounding, balance
Pranamaya	Vital energy	Vitality, radiance, flow
Manomaya	Mind & emotions	Mental clarity, peace
Vijnanamaya	Inner intelligence	Discernment, higher awareness
Anandamaya	Bliss, pure being	Liberation (Moksha), unity

This inner pilgrimage dissolves the outer identities and returns the seeker to their true nature — the witness, the unchanging consciousness that exists beyond all sheaths.

Integrating Practices for All Five Koshas

A complete yogic path involves addressing and nurturing all five layers:

Practice	Kosha
Yoga Asanas	Annamaya (Physical)
Pranayama, Energy Practices	Pranamaya (Vital)
Mantra, Mindfulness, Ritual	Manomaya (Mental)
Self-inquiry, Scriptural Study	Vijnanamaya (Wisdom)
Bhakti, Meditation, Stillness	Anandamaya (Bliss)

Each practice acts as a key that unlocks the gate to the next inner realm.

Beyond the Koshas

The goal of yoga is not merely mastery of the body or the calming of the mind. It is to become fully conscious of all five sheaths, purify them, and eventually transcend them — arriving at the Atman, the eternal Self beyond name, form, and experience.

As one ancient yogic teaching puts it:

"You are not the body.
You are not even the mind.
You are the blissful witness of it all."

To know the Koshas is to know the layers that obscure the Self — and to peel them back, one by one, is the essence of liberation.

CHAPTER 21
PANCHA BHUTAS - THE 5 ELEMENTS OF YOGIC ALCHEMY

In the vast and subtle terrain of Yogic science, few teachings are as foundational and transformative as the Pancha Bhutas — the Five Great Elements. Known to ancient seers and siddhas as the very building blocks of the cosmos, these elements are not simply material or symbolic—they are vibrational realities, energetic archetypes, and the essential constituents of life itself.

Whether we look to Yoga, Ayurveda, Siddha medicine, Tantric rituals, or Vedic cosmology, the same truth resounds: the human being is a microcosm (pinda) of the macrocosm (brahmanda). To understand the elements outside is to understand our inner architecture. To master them is to master our own evolution—physically, mentally, energetically, and spiritually.

What Are the Five Elements (Pancha Bhutas)?

The universe, in all its diversity, arises from the dynamic interplay of these five primordial energies:

Element	Sanskrit Name	Represents	In the Human Body	Energy Quality
Earth	*Prithvi*	Stability, foundation	Bones, tissues, skin	Heaviness, grounding
Water	*Apas*	Flow, cohesion	Blood, lymph, plasma	Coolness, adaptability
Fire	*Agni*	Transformation, radiance	Digestion, metabolism, vision	Heat, catalytic energy

| Air | *Vayu* | Movement, breath | Prana, nerve impulses | Lightness, mobility |
| Space | *Akasha* | Expansion, receptivity | Mind, sensory pathways | Vastness, subtle presence |

These elements are not metaphorical—they are energetic truths. Everything we see, touch, eat, think, and feel is composed of some combination of these five.

In the Yogic path, the goal is not just to understand them intellectually, but to harmonize them within ourselves through direct experience and embodied practice. This harmony is known as Bhuta Shuddhi — the purification of the elements.

What Is Bhuta Shuddhi?

Bhuta = Element

Shuddhi = Purification, refinement, alignment

Bhuta Shuddhi is a sacred internal technology — a method of aligning your elemental energies with the cosmic rhythm. It is not superstition; it is a systematic inner process. Just as an instrument must be finely tuned to produce harmonious music, so too must the five elements within us be balanced for the full flowering of life.

When the Elements Are Aligned:

- Your body becomes strong and radiant
- Your mind becomes still, focused, and joyful
- Your emotions are balanced and resilient
- Your energy flows freely, allowing deeper states of meditation
- Your consciousness opens to the higher dimensions

Bhuta Shuddhi is the preparation of the inner temple, making it fit for divine perception.

Yogic Insights into the Five Elements

Each element has its own nature, qualities, and spiritual impact. When they are in balance, we experience wholeness. When disturbed, they create physical illness, emotional imbalance, and spiritual disconnection.

Earth – Prithvi Tattva

The densest and most tangible element, Earth represents structure, stability, and endurance. It is the very ground of our physical existence.

- In the body: bones, tissues, hair, nails, skin
- If imbalanced: lethargy, rigidity, attachment, possessiveness

Yogic practices:

- Grounding asanas (e.g., Tadasana, Vrikshasana)
- Walking barefoot on natural ground
- Eating root vegetables and whole grains
- Earth-based rituals and offerings
- Earth teaches us to be rooted yet receptive, solid but not stagnant.

Water – Apas Tattva

Water is the principle of flow, emotion, and cohesion. It adapts, nourishes, and connects — both within and without.

- In the body: blood, lymph, urine, reproductive fluids

- If imbalanced: emotional volatility, cravings, edema, mucus buildup

Yogic practices:

- Hydrating with awareness (charged or copper-infused water)
- Abhyanga (oil massage)
- Ritual baths, flowing asana styles (e.g., Vinyasa)
- Chanting and singing (as water is linked to expression)

Water invites us to feel deeply, to let go, and to flow with grace.

Fire – Agni Tattva

Fire governs transformation, both physiological and psychological. It is the force of digestion, perception, and willpower.

- In the body: digestive system, eyes, body temperature, brain activity
- If imbalanced: anger, impatience, acid reflux, inflammation

Yogic practices:

- Surya Namaskar (Sun Salutation)
- Agnisara Kriya and digestive breathwork
- Sunbathing and fire rituals (Homa, Agnihotra)
- Spicy, warming herbs in moderation
  Fire helps us burn away illusion and ignite spiritual vision.

Air – Vayu Tattva

Air is the principle of movement and communication. It governs all dynamic processes in the body and mind.

- In the body: breath, nervous system, circulation, mental activity
- If imbalanced: anxiety, restlessness, dryness, fatigue

Yogic practices:

- Pranayama (especially Nadi Shodhana, Bhramari)
- Calming music and breath awareness
- Gentle wind exposure, swinging movements
- Light fasting and warm, oily foods

Air brings freedom, creativity, and sensitivity to life.

Space – Akasha Tattva

Space is the subtlest of the elements. It is the container for all other elements and is linked to awareness, sound, and spiritual expansion.

- In the body: mind, throat, sensory cavities, energetic field
- If imbalanced: disconnection, indecision, overthinking

Yogic practices:

- Meditation and silent sitting
- Mantra japa (chanting "OM," "HAM")
- Sky-gazing, time in open spaces
- Fasting and solitude

Space teaches us to listen, to receive, and to merge with the infinite.

Elemental Practices in Yogic Science

Yogis work with the elements through multiple layers of engagement:

1. Mantras for Bhuta Activation

Each element is linked to a specific bija (seed) sound:

- **Earth** – Lam
- **Water** – Vam
- **Fire** – Ram
- **Air** – Yam
- **Space** – Ham / Om

These sounds resonate with the elemental vibrations, purifying and awakening their energies in your body.

2. Asanas & Mudras

Postures and hand gestures directly influence elemental energies:

Element	Key Mudra	Effect
Earth	*Prithvi Mudra*	Strengthens stability and grounding
Water	*Varun Mudra*	Enhances hydration and fluidity
Fire	*Agni Mudra*	Boosts digestive and mental fire
Air	*Vayu Mudra*	Calms nervous system and anxiety
Space	*Shunya Mudra*	Increases spiritual receptivity

3. Food as Elemental Influence

The food you eat carries elemental signatures:

- ○ Spicy, pungent foods – stimulate Agni
- ○ Juicy fruits, liquids – nourish Apas
- ○ Root vegetables, grains – ground with Prithvi
- ○ Light, dry foods – increase Vayu
- ○ Fasting, minimalism – awaken Akasha

Eating with conscious awareness of elemental impact refines not just the body, but the entire energetic system.

Elemental Rhythms in Tamil Siddha Tradition

In the Tamil Siddha and Agamic sciences, time is cyclic, and the seasons and lunar cycles are expressions of elemental rhythms.

Tamil Month	Dominant Element	Spiritual Focus
Chithirai (Apr–May)	Fire (*Agni*)	Cleansing, transformation rituals
Aadi (Jul–Aug)	Water (*Apas*)	Emotional balance, inner surrender
Karthigai (Nov–Dec)	Fire + Space	Ideal time for deep spiritual sadhana

Temples, festivals, and sacred observances in Tamil culture are not arbitrary; they are aligned with elemental wisdom to optimize spiritual evolution.

Why Elemental Mastery Matters

Purpose of Balance	Yogic Benefit
Physical harmony	Health, strength, longevity
Mental clarity	Focus, serenity, resilience
Emotional regulation	Joy, love, compassion
Energetic purification	Pranic vitality and healing
Spiritual transcendence	Oneness, bliss, liberation (*moksha*)

You are not merely a personality or a body—you are a symphony of five sacred forces. The journey of yoga is to become conscious of these forces, to refine them through disciplined practice, and to finally transcend them, entering the pure awareness that is beyond all form.

"Master the elements, and nature itself becomes your ally. Purify the elements, and the Divine reveals itself through you."

PART IV
ENERGY, TEMPLES & THE SACRED SCIENCES

CHAPTER 22
THE CHAKRAS - WHEELS OF ENERGY, GATEWAYS TO THE INFINITE

The yogic science of Chakras is one of the most profound and transformative frameworks within the inner sciences of Yoga and Tantra. Far beyond metaphor or mysticism, chakras are real, experiential energy vortices—centers of life-force (prana)—that govern every dimension of our existence: from instinct to intellect, from survival to transcendence.

These energy centers serve as both maps and mechanisms for inner evolution. They are not anatomical organs, yet they directly influence the physical body, emotions, thought patterns, karmic memory, and spiritual perception. Balancing and awakening the chakras is not merely healing—it is liberation.

What Are Chakras?

The term Chakra (Sanskrit: चक्र) literally means "wheel" or "disc." In yogic science, it refers to a spinning vortex of energy located within the Pranamaya Kosha, the subtle energy body that lies beyond the physical form.

There are said to be seven primary chakras located along the Sushumna Nadi—the central energetic channel running parallel to the spine from the base to the crown of the head. Each chakra is an intersection point where nadis (energy channels) converge, and each serves as a portal between physical reality and higher consciousness.

Chakras:

Regulate vitality, emotions, and psychological states
Reflect spiritual maturity and karmic imprints
Act as bridges between the human and the divine

Purpose of Chakras in Yogic Science

In classical yoga and tantra, the purpose of understanding and working with chakras is not merely energetic balance, but conscious evolution. Chakras are like lenses through which we perceive reality—and through which reality flows into us.

Chakras serve four essential functions:

- **Transmit Life Energy (Prana)**: They draw cosmic energy into the system and distribute it to various physiological and subtle layers.

- **Store and Process Karma**: Each chakra is associated with distinct karmic themes—patterns and impressions from past experiences, both personal and ancestral.

- **Enable Spiritual Ascent**: As energy rises from lower to higher chakras, so does consciousness—moving from basic survival to divine unity (moksha).

- **Bridge the Physical and the Transcendent**: Chakras are junctions where body, mind, and soul communicate—offering a blueprint for holistic well-being and spiritual expansion.

The Seven Chakras – Their Essence and Role in Yogic Evolution

Each chakra governs specific physical organs, psychological traits, emotional tendencies, and spiritual capacities. Let us explore their essence:

1. Root Chakra – Muladhara

- Location: Base of the spine (perineum)
- Element: Earth
- Primary Function: Grounding, survival, physical security
- Awakening Brings: Stability, fearlessness, a strong foundation

Muladhara is the seat of survival instincts — our connection to the physical world. When balanced, it gives us a sense of being rooted, supported, and safe.

2. Sacral Chakra – Svadhisthana

- Location: Below the navel, in the pelvic area
- Element: Water
- Primary Function: Emotion, pleasure, creativity, sexuality
- Awakening Brings: Emotional flow, sensuality, freedom of expression

Svadhisthana governs our desires, emotions, and creative impulses. It allows us to experience life fully through sensation and feeling.

3. Solar Plexus Chakra – Manipura

- Location: Navel area, stomach
- Element: Fire

- ◦ Primary Function: Power, will, digestion, personal identity
- ◦ Awakening Brings: Confidence, inner strength, sense of purpose

Manipura is the center of self-esteem and determination. A strong Manipura chakra means having clear goals, strong willpower, and healthy boundaries.

4. Heart Chakra – Anahata

- ◦ Location: Center of the chest
- ◦ Element: Air
- ◦ Primary Function: Love, compassion, connection, emotional balance
- ◦ Awakening Brings: Unconditional love, empathy, acceptance

Anahata is where human connection deepens. It is the bridge between the lower (earthly) and higher (spiritual) chakras — turning love from attachment into divine compassion.

5. Throat Chakra – Vishuddha

- ◦ Location: Throat
- ◦ Element: Ether / Space
- ◦ Primary Function: Communication, truth, self-expression
- ◦ Awakening Brings: Clear expression, authenticity, powerful speech

Vishuddha helps us speak our truth and live authentically. It governs not just verbal expression but also integrity, honesty, and clarity of purpose.

6. Third Eye Chakra – Ajna

- ◦ Location: Between the eyebrows (brow center)

- ○   Element: Light / Mind
- ○   Primary Function: Intuition, inner vision, perception
- ○   Awakening Brings: Clarity, wisdom, spiritual insight

Ajna opens the gateway to inner knowing — intuition, imagination, and higher intelligence. It aligns us with inner vision and deep understanding.

7. Crown Chakra – Sahasrara

- ○   Location: Top of the head
- ○   Element: Beyond all elements (pure consciousness)
- ○   Primary Function: Unity, transcendence, spiritual liberation
- ○   Awakening Brings: Bliss, enlightenment, connection with the Divine

Sahasrara is the culmination of spiritual evolution — where the individual merges with universal consciousness. It is not just a chakra, but a portal to higher dimensions of being.

The Role in Yogic Evolution

The journey through the chakras mirrors the spiritual path:

- ○   We start at the root, learning to survive and stand firm.
- ○   We learn to feel, to express ourselves, and to own our power.
- ○   We expand the heart, become authentic, awaken insight, and finally…
- ○   We transcend the self, discovering we were never separate from the infinite.

Each chakra, when purified and awakened, opens new dimensions of human potential — leading from existence to essence, from form to freedom.

How Chakras Influence the Human Experience

Chakras are not abstract metaphors. They actively shape how we think, feel, act, and relate to the world. When a chakra is:

- Blocked or underactive, it can result in:
- Physical ailments
- Emotional disturbances
- Repetitive karmic patterns
- Balanced and open, it supports:
- Psychological harmony
- Emotional maturity
- Energy flow and intuition
- Awakened, it becomes a seat of spiritual power (siddhi)—a center of divine expression within the human body.

Example:

A constricted Anahata Chakra (heart) may show up as fear of love, emotional numbness, or difficulty forgiving.

A balanced Anahata flows as unconditional love, kindness, and healing.

How to Activate and Balance the Chakras

Yogic tradition offers an entire science of chakra sadhana—disciplined practice for awakening each center. These methods work on the body, mind, and energy simultaneously.

Practice	Purpose
Asanas (Postures)	Open and energize specific chakras
Pranayama (Breathwork)	Activate energy channels (nadis)
Mantra (Sound)	Tune to vibrational frequency of chakras

Meditation (Dhyana)   Bring conscious awareness to chakra space

Bandhas & Mudras   Redirect prana and stimulate psychic flow

Kundalini or Kriya Yoga   Direct energy ascent through Sushumna Nadi

Each chakra has associated seed mantras (bija mantras) and visual symbols (yantras, lotuses) used in meditative visualization and energy activation.

Kundalini and the Chakras: The Inner Ascent

At the base of the spine lies a dormant yet potent force called Kundalini Shakti—the coiled feminine energy of consciousness. When awakened, this primal force rises upward through the chakras, purifying, illuminating, and ultimately dissolving the egoic self.

As Kundalini pierces each chakra, it awakens higher potentials, and the yogi begins to perceive life with expanded awareness—seeing not just the world, but the divine principle within it.

This ascent is not metaphorical. It is a tangible, luminous experience achieved through deep yogic practice, grace, and inner stillness.

The Chakras as Inner Portals

Chakras are more than mystical ideas—they are gateways to the infinite. To journey through them is to journey through yourself. When understood and activated consciously, they become keys to physical health, emotional mastery, energetic balance, and ultimate liberation.

"Chakras are doors to inner worlds. When they open, the entire universe opens within you."

In the end, the awakening of the chakras is not about escaping the world but embracing it fully, consciously, and divinely—until the entire cosmos reveals itself within the subtle lotus of your being.

CHAPTER 23
CHAKRAS, THE TAMIL CALENDER & COSMIC ALIGNMENT - A SIDDHAR PERSPECTIVE

Within the yogic and Siddha traditions of South India, there exists a sacred science that interweaves the energy centers of the body (chakras), the cosmic calendar (Tamil months), and the rhythms of the universe. This is not a coincidence, but a living system of spiritual timing and inner transformation, precisely observed and practiced by ancient sages such as Agastya, Bogar, and Patanjali.

At its heart lies a fundamental truth of yogic philosophy:

"The human being is not separate from the cosmos. We are a mirror of the macrocosm."

Let us now unfold this timeless knowledge, layer by layer.

1. Chakras and Cosmic Timing – A Yogic Cosmology

In yogic understanding, chakras are not confined to the body—they are resonant fields that echo the very rhythms of the cosmos. They pulse with the movements of the sun, moon, and stars, cycling through periods of activation and rest, just as nature does.

The Tamil calendar, rooted in solar transit and nakshatra alignment, is more than a timekeeping system. It is a cosmic almanac, mapping the inner landscape of energy and evolution across twelve months—each correlating to a chakra and a phase in spiritual growth.

2. The Tamil Months and Their Yogic Resonance

The Tamil solar calendar begins with Chithirai (mid-April), marking the Sun's entry into Aries—symbolic of cosmic fire igniting life. Each month carries not just seasonal change, but a distinct vibrational signature, influencing the energy centers within us.

Tamil Month	Gregorian Months	Spiritual Theme	Chakra Resonance
Chithirai	Apr–May	New beginnings, grounding	Muladhara (*Root*)
Vaikasi	May–Jun	Rising solar force, awakening	Swadhisthana (*Sacral*)
Aani	Jun–Jul	Shiva's cosmic dance (*Ananda Tandava*)	Manipura (*Navel*)
Aadi	Jul–Aug	Divine feminine, surrender	Anahata (*Heart*)
Avani	Aug–Sep	Tapas (*discipline*), inner clarity	Vishuddha (*Throat*)
Purattasi	Sep–Oct	Dharma, order, devotion	Ajna (*Third Eye*)
Aippasi	Oct–Nov	Cleansing, release, rain	Ajna / Sahasrara
Karthigai	Nov–Dec	Inner light, illumination	Sahasrara (*Crown*)
Margazhi	Dec–Jan	Stillness, silence, sacred music	Beyond chakras (*Unity*)
Thai	Jan–Feb	Harvest, gratitude, returning inward	Return to Root
Maasi	Feb–Mar	Healing, reflection, purification	Chakra realignment
Panguni	Mar–Apr	Completion, divine union	Shiva–Shakti Oneness

Each month is not a point in time—but a step in a spiritual ladder. By moving through these months consciously, one traverses the chakra path, from earthly survival to cosmic realization.

3. The Chakras Reflecting Nature's Rhythms

The Sun's biannual movement—known in Vedic terms as Uttarayana (northern ascent) and Dakshinayana (southern descent)—deeply influences the chakras.

Uttarayana (Jan to Jun): The sun ascends; energy rises. This is the time for active sadhana, awakening, and transformation. Chakras are more easily activated.

Dakshinayana (Jul to Dec): The sun descends; energy turns inward. This is the season for devotion, reflection, and integration. Chakras are more readily stabilized and refined.

In yogic terms, the outer sun mirrors the inner prana. Thus, seasonal shifts are also shifts in subtle energy fields.

4. Siddhars, Time Portals & Energetic Gateways

Siddhars were not just mystics—they were celestial scientists. They observed that certain dates and star alignments open natural energetic gateways for transformation.

Events like Thai Poosam, Panguni Uthiram, and Karthigai Deepam are not just cultural rituals, but cosmic alignments—times when kundalini energy, Shakti, and grace can be accessed more powerfully.

These timings often correspond to nakshatra-chakra portals, where spiritual energy descends or ascends more easily.

Many South Indian temples were constructed with astronomical precision, aligned to these celestial markers, turning them into living energy devices.

5. Chithirai 1 – The Tamil New Year & Muladhara Activation

The Tamil New Year begins with Chithirai 1, when the sun enters Aries (Mesha Rashi), representing the birth of the solar current. It corresponds energetically to the Muladhara (root) chakra, the foundation of life and consciousness.

From there, each month symbolically activates the next chakra in sequence, culminating in Karthigai and Margazhi, which represent Sahasrara (crown) and transcendence beyond form.

This movement reflects the spiritual ascent of the yogi—from the density of matter to the silence of pure being.

6. How to Align with the Chakra–Calendar Connection

To live in harmony with this sacred alignment is to move with the flow of the cosmos. You can begin by synchronizing your spiritual practices with the energetic resonance of each month:

Practical Tools:

Chakra Mantras by Month

- LAM (Root – Chithirai)
- VAM (Sacral – Vaikasi)
- RAM (Solar – Aani)
- YAM (Heart – Aadi)
- HAM (Throat – Avani)
- OM (Third Eye – Purattasi)
- Silence / Sahasrara mantra (Karthigai–Margazhi)

Monthly Sadhana Themes

- Chithirai–Aani: Focus on prana, breathwork, grounding asanas
- Aadi–Purattasi: Practice devotion, japa, and mantra chanting
- Aippasi–Karthigai: Engage in inner rituals, contemplation, cleansing
- Margazhi: Embrace sacred sounds, early rising, deep silence

Temple Pilgrimage & Elemental Worship

Visit temples aligned with Pancha Bhutas (five elements), which also resonate with chakra energy:

- Earth – Kanchipuram (Ekambareswarar)
- Water – Tiruvanaikaval (Jambukeswarar)
- Fire – Tiruvannamalai (Arunachaleswarar)
- Air – Srikalahasti
- Space – Chidambaram

The Spiritual Ladder of Time

"The Tamil months are not just time markers—they are spiritual ladders that take your energy from the Earth to the Infinite."
— Siddhar Agastya, as preserved in ancient palm leaf texts

This knowledge invites you not only to observe time, but to live time spiritually. To flow with nature's current. To let each month unfold within you as an inner season, guiding your chakras, aligning your breath, and opening your being to the boundless cosmic rhythm.

CHAPTER 24
TEMPLES - ENERGY MACHINES OF THE ANCIENT YOGIC WORLD

In the vast expanse of Indian spiritual wisdom, few symbols are as enduring and misunderstood as the temple. To the casual observer, a temple may seem like a place of worship, devotion, or ritual. But to the yogi, to the Siddha, to the rishi who sees beyond the material — a temple is a living energy body. It is not a religious monument but a sacred instrument designed for inner transformation.

Temples, especially in the Vedic and Siddha traditions, were never meant to serve the purpose of blind worship. They were built as cosmic mechanisms — to align the individual with the universal, the physical with the metaphysical, and the seeker with the Source.

1. Why Were Temples Built? – The Yogic Vision

In their truest sense, temples were not created for prayer. They were created to elevate consciousness, to assist people in reaching higher states of inner balance, clarity, and transcendence. These sacred structures were built as yantras in stone, functioning like spiritual technologies:

- To purify human energy fields
- To awaken dormant faculties of perception
- To provide access to cosmic intelligence
- To act as energetic sanctuaries that nurture individual and collective wellbeing

"A temple is not a place to pray to God. It is a device to raise your energies beyond the limitations of the physical."

In ancient India, not everyone had the capacity or lifestyle to engage in deep meditation or tapas. Temples offered the common man and woman a glimpse of the divine through carefully designed architecture, rituals, and energized forms — creating an inner shift without intellectual effort.

2. The Origins of Temple Science

The concept of a temple emerges from the deep integration of yogic insight, Vedic cosmology, and spiritual engineering. Its foundational sources are:

- **Yogic science**: Understanding of the subtle body, energy centers (chakras), prana, and spiritual anatomy.
- **Agama Shastras**: Scriptural texts detailing sacred temple construction, idol consecration, and ritual alignment.
- **Vastu Shastra**: The science of spatial energetics — harmonizing structure, direction, and flow of energy.
- **Siddha and Tantric traditions**: Mastery over energy, mantra, and form to create living deities within inert matter.

In essence, a temple is a mirror of the human body. Just as the human body is a vehicle for consciousness, the temple is a body for cosmic energy to reside and radiate.

3. The Sacred Process of Temple Construction

The building of a temple was a sacred act — a collaboration between mystics, astrologers, sculptors, and architects, where every element was aligned with a specific intention.

Choosing the Location

Temples were never placed randomly. They were built upon natural energetic hotspots — places where:

∘ Earth's magnetic currents converged
∘ Underground water channels pulsed with vitality
∘ Subtle pranic vibrations were high

Rishis and yogis would detect these spaces through heightened perception, choosing only those lands that naturally supported the flow of higher energies.

Sacred Geometry and Alignment

Temples were designed using precise geometrical ratios that corresponded to cosmic patterns (like the Sri Yantra or Mandalas). Key features include:

∘ Square foundations symbolizing stability and grounding (Earth element)
∘ Alignments with cardinal directions and celestial movements (e.g., equinox sunrise falling directly on the sanctum)
∘ The Garbhagriha (sanctum sanctorum) placed at the energetic core, acting as the heart of the temple

Unlike modern buildings built for comfort, temples were built for energetic alignment — to subtly restructure your energy system as you walk through them.

Consecration – Infusing Life into Stone

Perhaps the most sacred step in temple creation is Prana Pratishtha — the act of infusing life-force into the idol. Through mantras, rituals, and deep meditative presence, the murti (idol) becomes a radiant center of shakti (energy). It's no longer a sculpture — it becomes a living presence.

Different temples serve different energetic functions:

- Shakti sthalas – feminine energy, transformation, healing
- Shiva sthalas – ascension, transcendence, liberation
- Vishnu sthalas – preservation, stability, harmony

4. Temple Symbolism – The Sacred Anatomy

Every aspect of a traditional temple is deeply symbolic, reflecting cosmic truths through architectural language:

Temple Part	Spiritual Symbolism
Gopuram (tower)	The spine or sushumna — the journey upward
Garbhagriha	The cosmic womb, inner sanctum, soul space
Kalasha (spire)	The sahasrara (crown chakra) — the divine union
Prakara (walls)	Boundary of energy — subtle containment
Nandi (bull)	Patience and alert stillness before awakening

A true devotee approaches the temple not merely with offerings, but with intent and receptivity. Every step is a ritual of internal realignment:

- **Removing footwear** – disconnecting from earth distractions
- **Circumambulation (Pradakshina)** – moving with the energy vortex
- **Offering flowers or lamps** – participating in energy exchange
- **Standing still before the deity** – to receive transformation

5. Temples and the Chakras – Inner Resonance

Temples are not only structured like the human body — they are energetically mapped to the chakras. Each major temple, especially in South India, vibrates with the resonance of a specific energy center:

Temple	Chakra Correspondence
Kanchipuram	Muladhara (*Root chakra*)
Thiruvannamalai	Ajna (*Third Eye chakra*)
Chidambaram	Sahasrara (*Crown chakra*)

By visiting these temples consciously, the devotee can activate and harmonize that corresponding chakra — without needing to intellectualize or visualize. The temple does the work. You simply need to be present and open.

6. Temples Then and Now – A Shift in Purpose

In ancient times:

- Temples were entered only by those spiritually prepared
- Priests were often siddhas or yogic adepts, trained in energy mastery
- Silence was the norm — rituals were performed for transformation, not tradition

In modern times:

- Temples have become cultural and religious centers
- Crowds, noise, and ritual repetition often overshadow inner experience
- Yet, a few ancient temples still retain their original power — places like Chidambaram, Arunachala, Kedarnath, and Meenakshi Amman remain vibrationally potent

It is up to the seeker to approach these spaces with the right awareness, reviving their original purpose.

The Temple as a Yogic Tool

Aspect	Essence
Purpose	To serve as a living yantra for energy transformation
Origin	Designed by rishis using yogic vision, Vastu, and Agamas
Function	To purify the individual, uplift the collective, and connect with the cosmos
Experience	One doesn't "pray" — one aligns, absorbs, and evolves

"A true temple is not a place to believe. It is a place to become."

Temples, when approached with sensitivity, are not structures of stone — they are gateways to the infinite. They hold the memory of the cosmos, encoded in silence and sacred vibration, waiting for the one who enters not with words, but with wonder.

CHAPTER 25
SACRED MACHINES OF CONSCIOUSNESS - THE SECRET YOGIC SCIENCE OF SOUTH INDIAN TEMPLES

In the heart of Southern India stand towering temples — majestic, intricate, alive. While many see them as grand architectural wonders or historical monuments, their true significance runs far deeper. These ancient South Indian temples — especially Chidambaram, Brihadeeswara, and Arunachaleswarar of Thiruvannamalai — are not merely places of worship. They are living energy systems, built with profound yogic knowledge and cosmic intent.

Designed by Siddhars, rishis, and enlightened rulers, these temples are spiritual technologies — encoded in stone — to mirror the cosmos and awaken the inner universe of the seeker.

Temples as Embodied Cosmos: Sacred Science in Stone

1. Temples Were Constructed Like the Human Body

In the wisdom of yogic science, the human body is seen as the first temple. And temples, in turn, were built to reflect the human subtle system — with chakras, energy flows, and spiritual anatomy.

Temples were conceived as a yogic body lying on its back, with each part representing a corresponding human organ or energetic center:

Temple Part	Symbolic Meaning	Human Body Equivalent
Gopuram (*Entrance*)	Gateway to inner being	Feet
Mandapam (*Corridor*)	Transition into sacredness	Legs and torso
Garbhagriha (*Sanctum*)	Womb of consciousness	Head and brain
Vimana (*Tower above*)	Cosmic antenna	Sahasrara (*Crown chakra*)

As the devotee walks inward from the bustling world outside, their journey mirrors the kundalini's ascent — from base (Muladhara) to crown (Sahasrara). This is not a metaphor. The energetic architecture of these temples creates a subtle transformation for those who walk with awareness.

2. What Is Prana Pratishtha? The Alchemy of Life in Stone

The idol, or murti, enshrined within the sanctum is not merely a sculpture. In its raw form, it is lifeless matter. But through Prana Pratishtha — the ancient science of consecration — it becomes a living, radiant being.

Yogis and priests, trained in Agama Shastra and subtle energy sciences, would infuse life into the idol using:

- Mantras – vibrational frequencies attuned to divine consciousness
- Mudras – sacred hand gestures channeling energy flow
- Pranayama and intention – breath merged with awareness
- Ritual geometry – placement aligned with cosmic laws

Once consecrated, the murti becomes an energetic battery — radiating waves of stillness, clarity, and transformation. To stand before it is not simply devotion — it is to be in the field of an awakened presence, much like sitting in the aura of a yogi in deep samadhi.

3. Three Sacred Temples and Their Mystical Architecture

Let us now explore three of South India's most powerful temples — not through history books, but through the lens of yogic mysticism and inner transformation.

Chidambaram Temple – The Temple of Space (Akasha)

"Chidambara Rahasya" – The Secret of the Cosmic Void

- Deity: Lord Nataraja (Dancing Shiva)
- Element: Akasha (Space/Ether)
- Chakra Connection: Sahasrara (Crown Chakra)

This temple is unlike any other. In its innermost sanctum, there is no visible deity — only empty space, draped in a golden curtain. This emptiness is not absence — it is presence in its most refined, unmanifest form.

Here, Shiva is not worshipped as form, but as pure formlessness — the Chid Akasha, or conscious space from which all creation emerges and dissolves.

Mystical Design:

- The golden roof (Chit Sabha) symbolizes the field of divine awareness.
- The entire layout is modeled on human anatomy, with the sanctum placed in the head region.
- Five sabhas (halls) represent the five koshas (layers of human existence).

To stand in Chidambaram is to be reminded that the ultimate temple is within, and that space itself is sacred.

Arunachaleswarar Temple – The Temple of Fire (Agni)

"Arunachala is not a mountain you visit — it is Shiva you merge with."

○ Deity: Lord Shiva as Arunachala

○ Element: Agni (Fire)

○ Chakra Connection: Ajna (Third Eye Chakra)

Thiruvannamalai is no ordinary site. The hill itself is revered as a formless linga, and the temple is an extension of its energy. It is said that just being near this mountain can ignite the fire of awareness within. Here, fire is not just physical — it is jnana agni (the fire of spiritual knowledge) that burns ignorance and karma.

Spiritual Highlights:

○ Ramana Maharshi, one of the greatest sages of modern times, attained self-realization at this very hill — through silence and inner inquiry.

○ The practice of Girivalam (14 km circumambulation of the hill) aligns the body to the fire element — dissolving karmic patterns.

This is a temple not for prayer, but for pure presence. It is a beacon for those ready to awaken the inner flame.

C. Brihadeeswara Temple – The Temple of Cosmic Balance

○ Deity: Lord Shiva as Brihadeeswara (The Great Lord)

○ Built by: Raja Raja Chola (11th century)

○ Element: Earth and Cosmic Order

○ Chakra Connection: Muladhara to Sahasrara

This temple is a masterpiece of Vastu and sacred geometry. Its towering Shikhara, carved from a single 80-ton stone, defies even modern engineering logic. No shadow of its dome touches the ground at noon — a design that symbolizes the timelessness and stillness of Shiva.

Yogic Insights:

- Built entirely without mortar — each stone interlocks, reflecting eternal unity.
- The central linga radiates massive energy, said to influence the entire region's pranic field.
- Measurements and proportions are based on cosmic mathematics and planetary rhythms.

Brihadeeswara is not just a symbol of power — it is a temple of perfect harmony between man, earth, and cosmos.

4. The Deeper Yogic Principles Embedded in Temple Design

Yogic Principle	Temple Expression
Kundalini Awakening	Journey from entrance (base) to sanctum (crown)
Chakra Alignment	Temple structure mirrors energy centers of the body
Shiva *(Stillness)*	Deity remains unmoving — reflecting the still mind
Darshan *(Seeing)*	Energetic transmission, not visual stimulus
Silence	Original temples had no loud music — only sacred stillness

Temples were created to help the aspirant move from doing to being, from seeking to seeing.

5. Why Circumambulation (Pradakshina) Matters

When you walk clockwise around a deity or sacred hill, your body aligns with the natural energy flow — which is also clockwise.

This practice:

- Harmonizes your bio-energetic field with the temple's frequency
- Cleanses and resets your subtle body
- Creates a meditative rhythm, anchoring awareness in the present moment

Girivalam at Arunachala, for instance, is not ritual — it is a living sadhana.

6. From Worship to Direct Experience

The purpose of a temple is not to believe — it is to become. Ancient temples were not built to demand faith but to trigger experience. They function as:

- Energy fields rather than sermon halls
- Inward journeys rather than outward performances
- Silent teachers rather than spoken preachers

This is why many yogis never spoke in temples — because the temple did the speaking through vibration and presence.

Temples as Inner Portals

Temples are not places to go and ask.

They are sacred fields to:

- Get aligned with the cosmos
- Sit in stillness and absorb
- Awaken dormant energies
- Dissolve the boundaries of self
- Realize that the divine is not separate from you

"If you know how to be in the presence of a consecrated space, you can know the divine — without ever reading a book, chanting a mantra, or lighting a lamp."

To the awakened eye, every temple whispers the same truth:

You are the sanctum. You are the fire. You are the space where Shiva dances.

CHAPTER 26
MAHA SHIVARATRI - THE NIGHT OF STILLNESS, THE GATEWAY TO THE INFINITE

Maha Shivaratri — often mistaken as just another religious observance — is, in truth, one of the most profound nights in the yogic calendar, revered not for external celebration, but for its energetic significance, cosmic alignment, and potential for inner transformation.

In yogic science, this sacred night is not merely cultural or mythological. It is a powerful spiritual opportunity — a cosmic window where the human system is naturally aligned to touch higher states of consciousness, making it a night unlike any other.

Let us explore this sacred night layer by layer:

1. What is Maha Shivaratri, Really?

The term Maha Shivaratri means "The Great Night of Shiva." But Shiva, in the yogic context, is not merely a deity seated on a mountain with matted hair and a trident. Shiva is the Adiyogi, the first yogi — the one who first explored and transmitted the science of consciousness.

More deeply, Shiva represents the formless, infinite void — that which is not, and yet from which everything arises. In yogic terminology, Shiva is the embodiment of absolute stillness — Shunyata — the silent, unmoving source behind all movement.

Maha Shivaratri is not a festival of lights or colors.
It is a night of profound stillness, inwardness, and spiritual receptivity.

On this night, seekers do not celebrate — they dissolve.

2. The Cosmic Alignment Behind Maha Shivaratri

Astronomical and Energetic Significance:

Maha Shivaratri occurs on the 14th night of the waning moon, just before the new moon (Amavasya), in the month of Maagha or Phalguna (February–March). This is the darkest night of the month, but in yogic understanding, darkness is not a negative force — it is the source of all creation.

On this night:

- The gravitational forces, lunar position, and planetary alignment create a natural upward pull in the human energy system.
- The Earth's energy supports the rise of prana (life force) through the central energy channel (Sushumna Nadi) in the spine.
- Spiritual practices become more potent — as subtle energy pathways are more active and the veil between dimensions is thinner.

Hence, staying awake and upright throughout the night is not symbolic — it is a deliberate yogic act to allow the energy to rise without resistance.

3. Why Yogis Revere This Night

For yogis and mystics, Maha Shivaratri is not a religious occasion — it is the peak of spiritual potential in the natural cycle.

On this night:

- The chakras become more sensitive and active

- ° Kundalini shakti, the dormant spiritual energy at the base of the spine, is more readily available to ascend
- ° The mind becomes quieter, and inner stillness more accessible
- ° The barrier between body, mind, and cosmic energy thins

It is said that Adiyogi himself entered complete stillness on this night — a moment of total absorption (nirvikalpa samadhi). This is why it is regarded as a night where one can experience deep meditative states, and even touch liberation (moksha) if approached with awareness.

4. The Yogic Science of What Happens Within

Yogic tradition doesn't merely rely on belief — it is rooted in observation of the inner system. Maha Shivaratri marks a time when the following changes occur naturally within:

- ° The Sushumna Nadi becomes more receptive, allowing prana to flow upwards
- ° The pineal gland, associated with intuition and the Ajna chakra, is more easily activated
- ° The body's alignment with gravity shifts, allowing energy to move vertically rather than stagnate at lower centers

Hence, the ancient instruction to stay awake, alert, and meditative throughout the night is not a ritualistic rule — it is an energetic alignment strategy.

"This is not a night to ask. This is a night to dissolve."

5. How to Approach Maha Shivaratri — The Yogic Way

You don't need elaborate rituals, fanfare, or temple visits. Maha Shivaratri is an inward celebration. The true observance is done in silence, stillness, and meditative awareness.

Preparations (Before the Night):

- Eat lightly or fast — to keep the system light and open
- Practice yoga asanas, pranayama, or Shoonya (emptiness) meditation
- Cleanse your physical space and set a clear inner intention: "May I transcend my limitations tonight."

On the Night:

- Stay awake (Jagaran) — resisting sleep is symbolic of overcoming tamas (inertia)
- Sit upright for as long as possible — aligning your spine is key
- Chant "Om Namah Shivaya", "Shiva Shiva", or simply remain in inner silence
- Practice meditation, breath awareness, or mantra repetition
- Join live satsangs, group meditations, or simply sit in conscious stillness

The posture of the body, clarity of the mind, and purity of intention are the real tools of the night.

6. Symbolism of Maha Shivaratri: A Journey into the Self

Symbol	Deeper Meaning
Darkness	The primordial womb — the source of all creation
Shiva	Formless awareness, transcendence, cosmic stillness

Staying Awake   Inner vigilance, awareness over the unconscious

Meditation   Uniting with the Absolute beyond body and mind

No rituals   Letting go of external, embracing the internal

Maha Shivaratri invites you to enter the mystery — not through intellect, but through experience. It is the night where you are the seeker, the path, and the destination.

A Night of Inner Alchemy

Maha Shivaratri is not an event on the calendar — it is a portal in consciousness.

It is a night to:

- Dissolve the identity
- Burn the karmic residue
- Touch the realm of Shiva — the infinite, the unborn, the unchanging

Even a single Shivaratri spent in true awareness, in inner silence, with intention and devotion, can leave you transformed from within.

"To be awake on this night is to be available to the grace of Shiva — not as a god outside, but as the stillness within."

Let this be not a night of worship, but a night of becoming — becoming Shiva, the one who is unmoved by time, untouched by fear, and unborn by nature.

CHAPTER 27
MANTRAS - THE SACRED SOUND CURRENT OF TRANSFORMATION

In yogic traditions, mantras are not merely words or sounds — they are sacred vibrations, each imbued with profound spiritual, psychological, and energetic significance. These powerful syllables and phrases act as portals that connect the practitioner to the universe, aligning body, mind, and spirit with higher states of consciousness. In essence, mantras are tools of inner transformation, creating harmony between the individual and the cosmos.

For millennia, yogis have harnessed the power of specific mantras not just as prayers or chants, but as vibrational keys that unlock hidden potentials within the practitioner's being. By repeating these sacred sounds, yogis have been able to awaken dormant energies, align themselves with universal forces, and attain profound states of spiritual realization.

Let us delve deeper into the most widely revered mantras, exploring their meaning, purpose, and the profound insights they offer on the path to self-realization.

1. AUM (ॐ) – The Primordial Sound of Creation

Mantra: *AUM*

Meaning: The primordial sound of the universe; it represents the union of body, mind, and spirit, the essence of creation itself.

Purpose and Use:

AUM is the most powerful and universal of all mantras, often referred to as the sound of the cosmos. It is the vibration from which all existence emanates and into which it ultimately dissolves. Chanting AUM is said to balance all chakras, calm the mind, and establish a direct connection to universal consciousness.

Yogic Insight:

Yogis believe AUM is not just a word — it is the very sound of creation, the primal vibration that reverberates through all of existence. Each sound within AUM symbolizes different states of consciousness:

A (अ) — Jagruti (Wakefulness): This represents the waking state of consciousness, where the individual experiences the world in its gross form.

U (उ) — Svapna (Dream State): The second sound represents the dream state, where consciousness is still active but in a subtler form.

M (म) — Sushupti (Deep Sleep State): The final sound represents deep sleep, where consciousness merges with the unmanifest and is dormant yet still existent.

Creation is seen by yogis as a cycle, beginning with the awakening of the formless Shiva principle, followed by the "dream" state where planets and organisms take form, and finally returning to the state of deep slumber, where all creation dissolves back into the formless void. Chanting AUM brings the practitioner into direct alignment with this cosmic rhythm, enabling them to transcend the limitations of individual identity and merge with the universal consciousness.

2. So Hum (सो ऽहम्) – "I Am That"

Mantra: *So Hum*
Meaning: "I am That" — a declaration of the unity between the self and the cosmos.

Purpose and Use:

This mantra is most commonly used in breath meditation. As you inhale, you silently chant So; as you exhale, you chant Hum. The mantra serves as a powerful tool to realize the self as part of the universal Self, dissolving the illusion of separation between the individual and the universe.

Yogic Insight:

The mantra So Hum points directly to the fundamental truth of non-duality. By repeating this mantra, the practitioner reminds themselves of their true nature — they are not separate from the universe, but one with it. The ego, which often reinforces the idea of individuality, is dissolved in the resonance of this mantra, revealing the interconnectedness of all existence.

3. Om Namah Shivaya (ॐ नमःशिवाय) – I Bow to Shiva

Mantra: *Om Namah Shivaya*

Meaning: "I bow to Shiva," symbolizing reverence for the inner Self — the still, transcendent consciousness that exists within each of us.

Purpose and Use:

This mantra is used to purify karma, awaken consciousness, and deepen self-realization. It is a powerful tool for spiritual awakening, acting as a key to unlock the dormant energy within the practitioner, particularly the kundalini energy.

Yogic Insight:

While Shiva is often revered as a deity, yogis understand Shiva as the ultimate state of consciousness, representing stillness, consciousness, and liberation. Chanting Om Namah Shivaya is an invocation of that stillness, enabling the practitioner to connect with the deepest layers of their being. This mantra activates spiritual energy, and through repeated chanting, it can awaken the dormant kundalini, allowing the practitioner to move toward enlightenment.

4. Gayatri Mantra – The Invocation of Divine Light

Mantra:

Om Bhur Bhuvah Swaha
Tat Savitur Varenyam
Bhargo Devasya Dhimahi
Dhiyo Yo Nah Prachodayat

Meaning: "We meditate on the divine light of the Sun (Savitur); may it inspire our inner vision."

Purpose and Use:

The Gayatri mantra is a powerful invocation of divine light, used to enhance wisdom, clarity, and spiritual insight. It is traditionally chanted to awaken higher intelligence (buddhi) and deepen meditative insight, often used in the morning to align the body and mind with the cosmic forces of nature.

Yogic Insight:

The Gayatri mantra is considered to be the essence of the Vedas, and its vibration is said to activate the third eye (Ajna chakra), opening the practitioner to higher states of awareness. Yogis chant this mantra to awaken the divine light within, dispelling ignorance and enhancing clarity of vision — not just in the physical world, but in the spiritual realm as well.

5. Mahamrityunjaya Mantra – The Mantra for Immortality

Mantra:

Om Tryambakam Yajamahe Sugandhim Pushtivardhanam
Urvarukamiva Bandhanan Mrityor Mukshiya Maamritat

Meaning: "We worship the three-eyed one (Shiva), who nourishes all beings. May He liberate us from the bondage of death, and grant us immortality."

Purpose and Use:

This mantra is a healing prayer, used to overcome the fear of death, transform negative karma, and receive spiritual protection. It is also chanted to achieve longevity and freedom from death and suffering.

Yogic Insight:

The Mahamrityunjaya mantra is considered one of the most sacred mantras for liberation from the fear of death. By invoking the three-eyed Shiva, the practitioner is seeking the spiritual energy of renewal and immortality. This mantra helps heal the body, mind, and spirit, dissolving the illusion of death and awakening the realization that the soul is immortal.

6. Ham Sa (हंसः) – The Sound of the Breath

Mantra: *Ham* (inhale), *Sa* (exhale)

Meaning: "I am That." Similar to So Hum, but linked to the natural rhythm of the breath.

Purpose and Use:

This mantra is intimately connected to the breath, as it naturally arises during the inhalation and exhalation process. It is a silent mantra, used to deepen breath awareness and promote inner stillness.

Yogic Insight:

The mantra Ham Sa is a natural mantra of non-duality, occurring in every living being. It is a subtle reminder that the self is not separate from the universe. In deep meditation, yogis become aware of this inner mantra, using it to dissolve the sense of separation and merge with the infinite cosmic presence.

7. Shiva Panchakshari – The Five Elements of Creation

Mantra: *Na Ma Shi Va Ya*

Meaning: Each syllable represents one of the five elements:

Na — Water
Ma — Earth
Shi — Fire
Va — Air
Ya — Ether (Space)

Purpose and Use:

This mantra is used in Shaivite practices to harmonize with the elements of creation, aligning the inner body with the outer world. It is a deeply transformative mantra, awakening inner stillness and liberation.

Yogic Insight:

By chanting Na Ma Shi Va Ya, the practitioner is symbolically invoking the five elements within their own body, purifying the physical and energetic body. This mantra connects the practitioner with the very source of creation, opening doors to cosmic consciousness and spiritual liberation.

Adiyogi — Shiva Himself — imparted this mantra to the Saptarishis (Seven Divine Sages), stating that if chanted with consciousness, it can open the doorways of the cosmos, allowing the practitioner to transcend the cycles of birth, death, happiness, and sorrow. By chanting this mantra with awareness, one can align themselves with the very rhythm of the universe.

How Yogis Use Mantras:

- **Repetition (Japa)**: Using a mala (prayer beads) to repeat the mantra 108 times.
- **Meditation**: Chanting aloud or silently during deep meditation.
- **Breath Coordination**: Syncing the mantra with the breath, such as in So Hum or Ham Sa.
- **Energetic Awakening**: Particularly with mantras like AUM or Om Namah Shivaya, which activate dormant spiritual energy.

Mantras are much more than just words. They are sound currents that reverberate through the universe, and through their repetition, the practitioner becomes aligned with the cosmic rhythm of life. Through mantra recitation, yogis achieve mental clarity, inner peace, spiritual awakening, and profound personal transformation.

Mantras are not just a means of communication with the divine — they are a powerful vehicle for transformation, helping the practitioner transcend the limitations of the mind and body, and align with the infinite consciousness that lies within and beyond.

PART V
THE PATH OF YOGA

CHAPTER 28
THE YOGA SUTRAS OF PATANJALI - A PATH TO LIBERATION AND ENLIGHTENMENT

The Yoga Sutras are a collection of 196 concise aphorisms or principles, attributed to the great sage Patanjali, compiled over 2,000 years ago. These sutras, which form the foundation of classical yoga philosophy, offer a profound exploration of the path to spiritual liberation. Through these timeless teachings, Patanjali provides a roadmap for the control of the mind, the purification of consciousness, and the ultimate goal of Moksha — liberation from the cycle of birth, death, and suffering.

The Yoga Sutras transcend the physical postures of yoga and encompass a complete system that integrates mental discipline, meditative practices, ethical conduct, and the cultivation of spiritual wisdom. They lay out the essence of yoga as a path of inner transformation and self-realization, guiding practitioners toward the experience of union with the Divine.

These 196 sutras are divided into four distinct chapters, or Padas, each of which addresses a unique aspect of the yogic journey. Together, they offer a comprehensive guide to the mastery over the mind, which is the ultimate aim of yoga, leading to the freedom of the soul.

The Structure of the Yoga Sutras

The four chapters (Padas) of the Yoga Sutras are as follows:

- **Samadhi Pada** — The Chapter on Meditation

- **Sadhana Pada** — The Chapter on Practice
- **Vibhuti Pada** — The Chapter on Powers
- **Kaivalya Pada** — The Chapter on Liberation

Each of these chapters elaborates on different facets of the yogic discipline, culminating in the highest goal of Kaivalya, the ultimate state of liberation and spiritual freedom. Let us explore each chapter in more detail:

1. Samadhi Pada: The Chapter on Meditation (Sutras 1-51)

The Samadhi Pada is the foundational chapter, focusing on the goal of yoga — to attain Samadhi, a state of deep meditative absorption. This chapter introduces the practitioner to the path of mental stillness, concentration, and the cultivation of higher states of consciousness. It is here that Patanjali lays out the primary goal of yoga: to still the fluctuations of the mind and achieve perfect concentration.

Key Insights from Samadhi Pada:

Yoga is the cessation of the fluctuations of the mind: The famous sutra "Yoga Chitta Vritti Nirodha" (Sutra 1.2) encapsulates the essence of yoga. Here, Patanjali emphasizes that yoga's true purpose is to calm the vrittis, or fluctuations, of the mind — the constant stream of thoughts, emotions, and distractions. Through yoga, we learn to still the restless mind and attain a state of deep peace.

Types of Samadhi: Patanjali describes various levels of meditative absorption, each more refined than the last. The highest state, Asamprajnata Samadhi, is where the meditator reaches pure consciousness, beyond thought, ego, and individuality. In this state, the individual experiences the oneness of all existence, transcending the limitations of the personal self.

The importance of detachment and regular practice: Patanjali underscores the need for two foundational practices: Vairagya (detachment) and Abhyasa (regular practice). Vairagya refers to the renunciation of attachments and distractions, while Abhyasa refers to disciplined and consistent practice. Both are essential for calming the mind and progressing on the path of meditation.

The five obstacles (Kleshas): The mind faces five primary obstacles, known as the Kleshas: Avidya (ignorance), Asmita (egoism), Raga (attachment), Dvesha (aversion), and Abhinivesha (clinging to life). These mental afflictions cloud our perception of reality and hinder spiritual progress. Overcoming them is an essential part of the yogic journey.

2. Sadhana Pada: The Chapter on Practice (Sutras 52-1.8)

The Sadhana Pada shifts the focus from the theoretical aspects of yoga to the practical and systematic practices that lead to the realization of Samadhi. This chapter outlines the Eightfold Path of yoga, known as Ashtanga Yoga, which provides a structured approach to cultivating discipline, wisdom, and self-awareness.

Key Insights from Sadhana Pada:

The Eight Limbs of Yoga (Ashtanga Yoga): One of the central teachings in this chapter is the Ashtanga Yoga, or the Eightfold Path, which consists of:

○   Yama (moral restraints)

○   Niyama (observances)

○   Asana (physical postures)

○   Pranayama (breath control)

○   Pratyahara (withdrawal of senses)

○   Dharana (concentration)

- Dhyana (meditation)
- Samadhi (absorption or enlightenment)

The role of the mind: Patanjali emphasizes the critical role of the mind in yoga practice. Through concentration (Dharana), meditation (Dhyana), and breath control (Pranayama), the practitioner learns to purify the mind and transcend distractions. It is through mental discipline that one is able to reach self-realization.

Kriya Yoga: Patanjali introduces the concept of Kriya Yoga, a practical form of yoga that purifies the body and mind through three core practices: Tapas (austerity or disciplined effort), Svadhyaya (self-study and reflection), and Ishvara Pranidhana (surrender to God or the Divine). These practices help the practitioner develop the inner strength necessary for meditation and self-realization.

Pranayama: Breath control is of paramount importance in this chapter. Through controlled breathing, one can regulate the flow of prana (life energy), calm the mind, and reduce mental distractions. Pranayama is an essential tool for deepening meditation and achieving mental clarity.

3. Vibhuti Pada: The Chapter on Powers (Sutras 1.5-1.22)

The Vibhuti Pada explores the extraordinary abilities, or siddhis, that may arise through diligent practice and meditation. These powers can include clairvoyance, telepathy, levitation, and even the ability to control the elements. However, Patanjali offers a cautionary note — these powers should not become distractions on the path to liberation.

Key Insights from Vibhuti Pada:

Siddhis: As a result of intense practice, a yogi may develop supernatural abilities, known as siddhis. These powers are signs of spiritual progress, but they can easily distract the practitioner from the ultimate goal of self-realization and liberation.

The danger of attachment: Patanjali warns that attachment to siddhis can lead to egoism and pride, causing the practitioner to lose sight of their true purpose. The ultimate aim of yoga is freedom from the ego, not the acquisition of powers.

Samyama: This concept is central to the development of siddhis. Samyama refers to the combination of Dharana (concentration), Dhyana (meditation), and Samadhi (absorption). Mastery of Samyama allows the practitioner to attain insight and siddhis, but Patanjali reminds us that these powers should not become an end in themselves.

4. Kaivalya Pada: The Chapter on Liberation (Sutras 1.23-1.34)

The final chapter of the Yoga Sutras, Kaivalya Pada, deals with the ultimate goal of yoga — Kaivalya, or liberation. In this state, the soul is freed from all limitations and the practitioner experiences union with the Divine. This chapter outlines the nature of self-realization and the ultimate state of freedom from the ego and material attachment.

Key Insights from Kaivalya Pada:

The nature of liberation (Kaivalya): Liberation is the state of complete freedom from the influence of the mind, the body, and the external world. In Kaivalya, the soul realizes its true nature — the eternal, unchanging self (Purusha) — and attains union with the Divine.

Viveka (discriminative wisdom): One of the essential tools on the path to liberation is Viveka, the ability to discern between the transient material world (Prakriti) and the eternal soul (Purusha). This wisdom enables the practitioner to detach from the distractions of the mind and realize their true nature.

Transcending the three gunas: The mind is influenced by three gunas (qualities): Sattva (purity), Rajas (activity), and Tamas (inertia). To reach liberation, one must transcend these gunas and go beyond the distractions of the material world, realizing the oneness of the soul with the universe.

The Yoga Sutras of Patanjali provide a complete philosophical framework for the practice of yoga, not merely as a series of physical postures but as a path to mental clarity, spiritual awakening, and ultimately liberation. Patanjali's teachings guide us in the process of purifying the mind, calming the senses, and transcending the limitations of the ego.

By practicing the principles outlined in these sutras, the practitioner gradually attains self-realization, experiencing union with the Divine and achieving the highest goal of yoga: Moksha — liberation from all suffering, and the realization of the true, eternal self. The Yoga Sutras provide a roadmap to a life of peace, wisdom, and ultimate freedom.

CHAPTER 29
THE PATH OF YOGA EXEMPLIFIED BY THE RISHIS OF ANCIENT INDIA

The great Rishis (sages) of ancient India were not just spiritual seekers; they were embodiments of distinct yogic paths, each exemplifying a unique approach to spiritual awakening. These paths were deeply rooted in the individual temperaments, life missions, and cosmic roles of the Rishis. By exploring their journeys, we can gain a profound understanding of the diverse methods through which one can seek union with the Divine, and the transformative power of these paths in the evolution of consciousness.

Each Rishi's path of yoga was more than just a personal discipline; it was a living example of how the sacred knowledge of the Vedas, the Upanishads, and the sutras could be integrated into daily life to help the individual transcend the limitations of the material world and experience the eternal Self. The Rishis offer us timeless guidance that continues to resonate deeply with spiritual aspirants across the world.

Rishis and Their Unique Paths of Yoga

Each Rishi's practice reflects their individual journey, yet all paths ultimately lead to the same goal: liberation (Moksha) and unity with the Divine. Let's explore the distinct yogic paths exemplified by some of the most revered Rishis:

Rishi Yajnavalkya — Jnana Yoga (The Path of Knowledge)

- **Focus:** Atma Vidya (knowledge of the Self), metaphysical inquiries, inner renunciation.
- **Text Reference:** Brihadaranyaka Upanishad.

- Known For: Yajnavalkya is renowned for imparting the deep wisdom of Advaita Vedanta (non-dualism) to King Janaka and his wife, Maitreyi, teaching them the ultimate truth of the Self beyond the body and mind.

- Essence: "The Self alone is to be known" – Yajnavalkya's teachings focus on self-inquiry and the realization that the individual soul (Atman) is one with the Universal Soul (Brahman). His path involves inner renunciation, transcending worldly attachments, and gaining wisdom through direct experience of the Self.

Through Jnana Yoga, Yajnavalkya guides us to seek wisdom not through external sources but through inner discernment, questioning the nature of reality and understanding that true knowledge comes from within. His teachings encourage an intellectual quest that transcends ordinary thinking and leads to the realization of our divine essence.

Rishi Vishwamitra — Karma Yoga → Raja Yoga → Brahma Rishi (The Path of Action and Meditation)

- Focus: Initially as a king, Vishwamitra embodied Karma Yoga (the yoga of selfless action), which later evolved into Raja Yoga (the path of meditation and control over the mind).

- Transformation: Vishwamitra's journey is one of extraordinary transformation—from a Rajarishi (king-sage) to a Brahmarishi (sage of the highest order) through intense tapas (spiritual discipline). His relentless dedication, overcoming the temptations and struggles of his royal life, exemplifies the path of inner awakening through perseverance.

- Known For: Composing the Gayatri Mantra—one of the most revered mantras in the Vedic tradition—and for creating the mythic Trishanku Swarga (a parallel heaven), Vishwamitra's life serves as a testament to human effort leading to divine realization.

- **Essence:** His path shows that human effort combined with spiritual discipline can lead to transcendence, bridging the material and spiritual worlds. Through the practice of Karma Yoga, Vishwamitra teaches us that action performed with a spirit of service leads to divine wisdom and liberation.

Vishwamitra's story exemplifies the potential for transformation through discipline and meditative insight, culminating in an experience of oneness with the divine.

Rishi Valmiki — Bhakti Yoga + Karma Yoga → Jnana Yoga (The Path of Devotion and Knowledge)

- **Focus:** Transformation through devotion and remembrance of Lord Rama, coupled with the performance of duty.
- **Known For:** Valmiki is best known for composing the Ramayana, the epic narrative of Lord Rama's life. His life illustrates the power of Bhakti Yoga (the path of devotion) in transforming a life from sin to sanctity, through deep emotional surrender and devotion to God.
- **Path:** Valmiki's journey begins with a life of sin, but through his deep devotion to Lord Rama, he transforms into a saintly figure. His practice blends Bhakti (devotion) with Karma (selfless action)—his writing of the Ramayana being both a sacred act of duty and a path of deep spiritual insight (Jnana Yoga).
- **Essence:** Valmiki's path teaches that devotion and sacred action are powerful tools for spiritual growth. By dedicating oneself to the Divine through both emotion and service, one can attain the highest state of wisdom.

Valmiki exemplifies how devotion and selfless service can lead to the realization of self-knowledge, with love as the key to inner transformation.

Rishi Patanjali — Raja Yoga (The Path of Meditation and Mind Mastery)

○ **Focus:** Mastery over the mind through meditation and self-discipline.

○ **Known For:** Patanjali is celebrated for systematizing the ancient practices of yoga in his Yoga Sutras, which outline the Eightfold Path (Ashtanga Yoga) as a means of attaining mental clarity, inner peace, and self-realization.

○ **Essence:** "Yoga is the stilling of the mind." – For Patanjali, Raja Yoga is the path to mental mastery. By practicing meditation (Dhyana) and mindfulness, the practitioner gradually stills the fluctuations of the mind, leading to a direct experience of the true self.

○ **Key Teaching:** Through the eight limbs of yoga (Yama, Niyama, Asana, Pranayama, Pratyahara, Dharana, Dhyana, Samadhi), Patanjali provides a complete framework for transforming the mind and achieving spiritual awakening. His emphasis on mental discipline and meditative practice offers us a structured path to inner peace and freedom.

Patanjali's path is one of self-mastery and mental purification, leading the practitioner to the ultimate realization of the self.

Rishi Agastya — Karma Yoga + Tantra Yoga + Siddha Science (The Path of Practical Spirituality)

○ **Focus:** Application of spiritual wisdom in daily life, encompassing healing, herbs, mantras, and Tantra.

○ **Known For:** Agastya is a multifaceted Rishi, credited with balancing the spiritual energies of the North and South of India, as well as spreading Siddha (esoteric) knowledge. He is often depicted as a sage who is deeply connected to the earth and its mystical forces.

○ **Essence:** Agastya's teachings exemplify the integration of spirituality with practical living. Through Tantra and Karma Yoga, he shows that service to others and mastery over the physical world (through mantras and healing practices) can lead to spiritual progress. His earth-based wisdom is rooted in an intimate understanding of nature and the universe.

Agastya's path teaches that the divine is not separate from the world around us. Service, healing, and the mastery of natural forces through Tantra lead to spiritual growth and realization.

Rishi Vasistha — Jnana Yoga (with Bhakti Undertones)

- **Focus:** Non-dual awareness, the realization of consciousness as the absolute.
- **Known For:** The Yoga Vasistha, a philosophical dialogue between the sage Vasistha and Sri Rama, explores the nature of reality, the mind, and the illusory nature of the world.
- **Essence:** Vasistha teaches that liberation comes through the realization that the world is an illusion (Maya) and that true knowledge lies in understanding the unity of all things. His teachings combine Jnana Yoga (the yoga of knowledge) with elements of Bhakti Yoga (the yoga of devotion), showing that the path of wisdom can also be imbued with love and devotion to the Divine.

Vasistha's wisdom teaches us to discriminate between the real and the illusory, ultimately realizing the absolute nature of consciousness.

Rishi Narada — Bhakti Yoga (The Path of Love and Devotion)

- **Focus:** The pure love for the Divine and spreading devotion.
- **Known For:** Narada is revered for his teachings on Bhakti through the Narada Bhakti Sutras. He is the eternal devotee of Lord Narayana and

is often depicted as spreading the message of devotion through divine music and song.

- ○ **Essence:** Narada teaches that love is the most powerful path to liberation. Through pure devotion and constant remembrance of the Divine, the soul can transcend all barriers and unite with God. "Where there is love, there is God" is his timeless message.

Narada's path is one of unconditional love, where the devotee surrenders their heart completely to the Divine.

Rishi Kapila — Sankhya Yoga (The Path of Analytical Discrimination)

- ○ **Focus:** Analysis of the nature of Purusha (spirit) and Prakriti (matter).
- ○ **Known For:** Kapila is credited with founding the Sankhya philosophy, which offers a rational, analytical framework for understanding the universe and the nature of the self.
- ○ **Essence:** Sankhya Yoga is an intellectual path of deep discrimination (Viveka), wherein the practitioner analyzes the distinction between consciousness and matter. Liberation comes through the realization that the true self (Purusha) is distinct from the physical body and mind, and that understanding this duality leads to freedom.

Kapila's path emphasizes analytical understanding as the key to spiritual liberation.

Rishi	Primary Yoga	Essence / Role
Yajnavalkya	Jnana Yoga	Knowledge of the Self
Vishwamitra	Karma → Raja → Jnana	Human effort & transcendence
Valmiki	Bhakti → Karma → Jnana	Devotion & transformation
Patanjali	Raja Yoga	Mental mastery, structured yogic path
Agastya	Karma + Tantra	Siddha science, applied spirituality
Vasistha	Jnana Yoga	Non-dual wisdom, illusion of the world
Narada	Bhakti Yoga	Pure love for the Divine
Kapila	Sankhya Yoga	Intellectual analysis of reality

Each of these Rishis offers a unique path that serves as an example for practitioners to follow in their own spiritual journeys. Whether through knowledge, devotion, meditation, or selfless action, the diverse approaches of the Rishis illustrate that there is no single way to liberation—only the path that aligns with the nature and temperament of the seeker.

CHAPTER 30
THE PATH OF THE YOGI - A JOURNEY INTO YOGIC PHILOSOPHY

As I step further into the realm of spirituality, I find myself drawn to a path that feels both grounded and experiential: Yogic Philosophy. Unlike some spiritual paths that demand unquestioning belief or adherence to dogma, yoga invites us into a world of direct experience—of conscious awareness and self-discovery. In many ways, it aligns seamlessly with where I left off in my exploration of science—consciousness, the most profound and mysterious aspect of existence.

But why yoga? The term "yoga" is often misunderstood in the West as merely a physical practice of postures, stretching, and flexibility. While these physical aspects are important, they are just the surface. The true essence of yoga is philosophical, and it offers us a profound science of the inner world—one that isn't about belief, but about direct experience. It challenges us not to accept ideas blindly but to observe, to experience, and to become conscious of ourselves, our thoughts, and our relationship to the universe.

This is a philosophy that does not impose itself but gently encourages us to awaken to our own truth.

What is Yogic Philosophy?

The term "yoga" comes from the Sanskrit root yuj, meaning "to unite" or "to yoke." But what exactly are we uniting?

At its core, yoga is the union of the individual self (atman) with the universal self (Brahman). In more modern terms, yoga is the merging of the limited "I"—our ego, our personality, our identity—with something far greater: pure awareness, the observer, the unchanging consciousness that is the essence of all being.

This is the essential teaching of Yogic Philosophy: we are not just our bodies, nor are we simply our thoughts and emotions. We are something far beyond—the witness, the self, the seer of all things. And in realizing this, we begin to transcend the illusion of separateness and return to our true nature, which is timeless, boundless, and ever-present.

This philosophy is not simply abstract; it is expressed through centuries of sacred texts that offer both insight and guidance on how to awaken to the deeper truths of life. Some of the foundational texts that lay out the principles of yoga include:

- **The Yoga Sutras of Patanjali**: A systematic guide to the process of inner transformation.
- **The Bhagavad Gita:** A dialogue between Lord Krishna and the warrior prince Arjuna, exploring the nature of the self, duty, and the path of devotion.
- **The Upanishads**: Ancient philosophical teachings that explore the nature of reality, consciousness, and the ultimate truth.

These texts do not preach or demand blind faith; instead, they guide us, step by step, on the journey from confusion to clarity, from chaos to calm, and ultimately, from ignorance to self-realization. They offer not answers, but tools to discover our own truth.

The 8 Limbs of Yoga (Ashtanga Yoga) – A Roadmap for the Inner Journey

One of the most revered systems in yogic philosophy is Ashtanga Yoga, the "Eight-Limbed Path" described by Sage Patanjali in his Yoga Sutras. Ashtanga Yoga serves as a roadmap for exploring and understanding the inner workings of consciousness, as well as a step-by-step guide to the process of spiritual evolution. Each of the eight limbs functions like a tool, carefully designed to help us transcend the limitations of the mind and connect with the true nature of our being.

The eight limbs are:

- **Yama – Ethical principles:** These are universal moral guidelines for living harmoniously with the world around us. They include ahimsa (non-violence), satya (truthfulness), and asteya (non-stealing), which guide us in our interactions with others.
- **Niyama – Self-discipline:** These are personal observances that promote inner cleanliness, contentment, and spiritual growth. They include shaucha (purity), santosha (contentment), and tapas (self-discipline).
- **Asana – Physical postures:** The practice of asana helps to prepare the body for stillness and meditation. Through physical practice, we cultivate strength, flexibility, and balance, both in the body and mind.
- **Pranayama – Breath control:** By controlling the breath, we learn to regulate the flow of prana (life force energy). Pranayama is a powerful tool for calming the mind and cultivating heightened awareness.
- **Pratyahara – Withdrawal of the senses:** This limb teaches us to turn inward, withdrawing our attention from external distractions in order to become more aware of our inner world.
- **Dharana – Focused concentration:** The practice of dharana trains the mind to focus on a single object, such as the breath, a mantra, or a visual image. This develops the ability to concentrate without distraction.

- ○ **Dhyana – Meditation:** Building on dharana, dhyana is the practice of maintaining an effortless, continuous state of awareness. It is meditation in its truest form, where the distinction between the meditator and the object of meditation begins to dissolve.

- ○ **Samadhi – Union, enlightenment:** This is the culmination of the yogic journey, where the practitioner experiences a profound state of oneness with the universe. It is a state of complete absorption in the self, where duality ceases to exist, and the practitioner realizes their identity with the absolute.

This eight-limbed path is not a linear process. Each step builds upon the last, creating a holistic, integrated approach to spiritual growth. It is both structured and logical, providing a clear framework for exploring the depths of the mind and spirit. But it is also deeply spiritual, guiding us toward a higher state of awareness and consciousness. Through these practices, we learn not only to live consciously but to experience transcendence and inner peace.

Where Yogic Philosophy Meets Science

What struck me deeply as I explored yoga is that it does not stand in opposition to science—it completes it. While science offers us tools to understand the material world, yoga delves into the mysteries of the inner universe, providing us with methods to explore the nature of consciousness itself.

In many ways, the realms of quantum physics and yogic philosophy converge at the very edges of our understanding of reality. As quantum physics explores the observer effect, non-locality, and the nature of consciousness, yoga begins its inquiry.

- ○ **The Observer Effect:** In quantum physics, the presence of the observer affects the observed phenomenon. In yoga, this corresponds to the seer, the conscious witness who perceives reality, yet is not bound by it.

- **Entanglement:** Quantum physics tells us that particles can be entangled, such that the state of one instantly affects the other, regardless of distance. In yoga, this is mirrored in the understanding of the unity of all beings—the recognition that at a deep, fundamental level, all of existence is interconnected.

- **Uncertainty:** In quantum physics, uncertainty is a fundamental principle that governs the behavior of particles. Yogic philosophy embraces this concept, teaching us to live with mystery, to surrender, and to let go of the need for rigid control. Through this surrender, we find true peace and freedom.

Yoga doesn't merely describe these phenomena; it offers practices—through meditation, breathwork, and self-inquiry—that allow us to experience them directly. In essence, yoga offers a practical, embodied approach to the very concepts that modern science is still grappling with.

Why This Matters Now

In the past, I sought truth outside of myself—through formulas, particles, and theories, looking for the essence of existence in the external world. Now, yoga has shifted my focus inward. It invites me to look not just at the outer world, but deeply within—to experience truth not as an intellectual concept, but as an embodied reality.

This is not about abandoning logic or reason; it is about deepening them. It is not about blind following, but about personal realization through direct experience.

As I begin this new chapter, I recognize that the path of the yogi is a path of awareness, transformation, and self-discovery. It's a journey that invites me to experience life more fully, to transcend the limitations of my individual ego, and to return to the vast, timeless consciousness that connects all of us.

CHAPTER 31
THE 8 LIMBS OF YOGA - A PATH TO SPIRITUAL LIBERATION

The 8 Limbs of Yoga, or Ashtanga Yoga, as outlined by the ancient sage Patanjali in his seminal work, the Yoga Sutras, offer a profound, holistic path to spiritual growth. These eight steps are not merely a series of physical postures or isolated practices. They represent a complete spiritual journey—a sacred map leading one from the external world of distractions and limitations to the deepest core of the inner Self.

While modern-day yoga is often synonymous with physical postures (asanas), Patanjali's Ashtanga Yoga is much more than that. It is a full spectrum of practices designed to purify and harmonize body, mind, and spirit, ultimately guiding the practitioner to a state of union with the Divine, or moksha (liberation).

Let us explore the 8 Limbs of this sacred path and the transformative potential they hold.

The 8 Limbs of Yoga (Ashtanga Yoga)

- **Ashta:** Eight
- **Anga:** Limbs / Parts
- **Together:** A unified approach to spiritual awakening and inner liberation.

The eight limbs of yoga form an integrated system, not just for physical health but for spiritual awakening. Each limb builds upon the other, and together they create a comprehensive framework that prepares us to experience our highest potential as human beings.

1. Yama: Ethical Restraints – Our Relationship with the World

The first limb of Ashtanga Yoga, Yama, is about how we interact with the world around us. These are the ethical principles that guide our actions, ensuring that we live in harmony with others and with the environment. Yama helps us refine our conduct, teaching us to act with integrity and respect for all living beings.

Yama is often referred to as "the don'ts"—the moral disciplines we follow to avoid harming others and ourselves. There are five Yamas:

- **Ahimsa (Non-violence):** This is the foundation of all ethical principles in yoga. It calls for kindness in thought, word, and action. Ahimsa teaches us to foster compassion and peace, not only towards others but also towards ourselves.

- **Satya (Truthfulness):** Living in alignment with truth, both in our speech and actions. Satya encourages us to speak the truth, but also to live the truth, to honor our integrity and honesty in all aspects of life.

- **Asteya (Non-stealing):** This goes beyond the act of stealing material possessions—it also refers to stealing time, ideas, or energy from others. Asteya invites us to live with generosity and to respect the boundaries of others.

- **Brahmacharya (Moderation/Celibacy):** The practice of self-control and balance, particularly in our desires. Brahmacharya teaches us to master our impulses, especially those that distract us from spiritual progress.

- **Aparigraha (Non-possessiveness):** Letting go of greed and attachment to material possessions. Aparigraha encourages us to embrace contentment, realizing that happiness does not come from accumulating things but from letting go of unnecessary attachments.

Purpose: Yama purifies our external life and relationships, creating the foundation for a peaceful, harmonious existence with others and the world around us.

2. Niyama: Internal Disciplines – Our Relationship with Ourselves

While Yama governs our external behavior, Niyama focuses on internal discipline—how we relate to our inner world. These practices promote self-purification, cultivating virtues that refine our character and strengthen our spiritual resolve. Niyama is referred to as "the do's," guiding us to consciously create a life that nurtures our growth.

The five Niyamas are:

- **Shaucha (Cleanliness):** Both outer and inner purity. Shaucha teaches us to maintain cleanliness in our body, mind, and surroundings, fostering an environment that supports spiritual practice.

- **Santosha (Contentment):** The practice of finding joy in the present moment, regardless of external circumstances. Santosha teaches us the power of acceptance and gratitude, encouraging us to feel content with what we have.

- **Tapas (Discipline):** Tapas refers to willpower, austerity, and mental fortitude. It is the inner fire that drives us to persevere through challenges, cultivating strength and resilience in our spiritual practice.

- **Svadhyaya (Self-study):** The study of sacred texts and self-reflection. Svadhyaya invites us to explore our inner world and learn more about our true nature through personal reflection and deep study.

- **Ishvarapranidhana (Surrender to God):** The act of letting go and surrendering to the Divine. This is the practice of devotion and humility, acknowledging that the path to spiritual liberation is guided by a higher power.

Purpose: Niyama cultivates inner clarity, strength, and devotion, allowing us to purify our minds and hearts, making us receptive to spiritual insights.

3. Asana: Postures – Preparing the Body for Stillness

The third limb, Asana, is what most people associate with yoga: the physical postures. However, in the context of Patanjali's teachings, asanas are not about flexibility or strength but about creating stability and comfort in the body to prepare for meditation. The ultimate goal of Asana is to develop a body that can sit still for long periods of time, cultivating the capacity for deep meditation.

Purpose: Asana develops physical discipline and creates the foundation for a still body and mind, allowing us to enter a state of meditation with ease.

4. Pranayama: Breath Control – Mastery of the Life Force

Pranayama is the practice of controlling the breath—an essential tool for controlling the mind. The word "prana" refers to the life force or vital energy that permeates all living things, while "ayama" means extension or control. Pranayama techniques involve regulating the breath through various methods, such as inhalation (Puraka), retention (Kumbhaka), and exhalation (Rechaka). By mastering the breath, we can master the mind and direct energy to fuel our meditation and spiritual progress.

Purpose: Pranayama helps calm the mind, energize the body, and prepare for deep meditation.

5. Pratyahara: Withdrawal of the Senses – Turning Inward

Pratyahara is the practice of withdrawing the senses from external distractions. It is the process of turning our awareness inward, detaching from sensory experiences and external stimuli that pull us away from the present moment. Pratyahara is often likened to a turtle withdrawing into its shell—an inner retreat where we no longer react to the external world but instead focus on the inner landscape.

Purpose: Pratyahara allows us to master distractions, creating a bridge between external practices and the inner journey of meditation.

6. Dharana: Concentration – Focused Attention

Dharana is the practice of focused concentration on a single object, such as the breath, a mantra, or a visual image. It is the ability to hold attention without wavering, training the mind to become steady and unwavering in its focus. Dharana is the precursor to meditation and essential for moving beyond the distractions of the mind.

Purpose: Dharana develops mental discipline, teaching the mind to remain still and focused.

7. Dhyana: Meditation – Effortless Awareness

Dhyana is the state of continuous flow of awareness. It goes beyond concentration to a place of deep absorption. Meditation is not about thinking of something; rather, it is about becoming absorbed in the object of meditation. In Dhyana, the distinction between the meditator and the object of meditation begins to dissolve.

Purpose: Dhyana dissolves the ego, allowing the practitioner to connect with higher consciousness and experience profound inner peace.

8. Samadhi: Absorption – Union with the Divine

Samadhi is the final stage of the yogic path, the ultimate goal of meditation. It is the state of complete absorption in the object of meditation, where the ego dissolves, and only pure awareness remains. There are two types of Samadhi:

○   **Savikalpa Samadhi:** A state of contemplation with thought.
○   **Nirvikalpa Samadhi:** A state of thoughtless absorption, where the individual merges with the Divine and transcends all duality.

Purpose: Samadhi represents the final liberation (moksha), the state of complete stillness, bliss, and oneness with the Divine.

The 8 Limbs of Yoga are not discrete steps to be climbed one after another. Instead, they are the limbs of one living tree, each part interconnected and nurtured together. As we cultivate these limbs—ethics, breath, body, and awareness—we move closer to the realization of our true nature and our union with the Divine.

CHAPTER 32
KUNDALINI & AWAKENING - THE RISING ENERGY, SYMBOLS, INNER EXPERIENCE

There is a profound energy within us, lying dormant, waiting to be awakened. I remember the first time I came across the concept of Kundalini — the coiled serpent energy that resides at the base of the spine. At that moment, it felt like discovering a secret force within, one that could shake the very foundations of my being. Little did I know, this energy was not just a concept, but an experience — an experience that would change everything.

Kundalini is often depicted as a serpent, coiled three and a half times at the base of the spine, symbolizing the potential power that lies untapped within us. It is the primal force, the energy of creation itself, linked to Shakti — the divine feminine energy, the source of all movement, change, and transformation in the universe. When this energy is awakened, it ascends through the chakras, the energy centers of the body, ultimately leading to the highest realization — union with the Divine.

But what does it mean for this energy to awaken? What happens when it rises? The truth is that the awakening of Kundalini is not just about experiencing a surge of energy. It is a complete transformation of consciousness, an evolution of the very way we perceive the world and ourselves. It is the beginning of an inner journey toward wholeness, where we shed layers of the ego and step into a higher state of being.

The Path of Kundalini Awakening

In the early stages, the experience of Kundalini awakening can be subtle — a sense of heightened awareness, an increased connection to the divine, a sudden clarity or insight into one's life purpose. But as the energy begins to rise, it can stir up deeper, more intense sensations. It can bring up unconscious fears, unresolved emotions, and past traumas that need to be purged in order for the energy to flow freely.

The Kundalini energy travels through the central channel, Sushumna, within the spine, moving upward through each chakra — the root chakra (Muladhara), sacral chakra (Svadhisthana), solar plexus (Manipura), heart chakra (Anahata), throat chakra (Vishuddha), third eye chakra (Ajna), and finally, the crown chakra (Sahasrara), located at the top of the head.

Each chakra represents a different aspect of our being. As the Kundalini rises through these energy centers, it awakens and purifies them. The root chakra represents our foundation and survival instincts, while the sacral chakra governs creativity and emotions. The solar plexus holds our personal power and will, while the heart chakra governs love and compassion. The throat chakra is the center of communication and expression, and the third eye governs intuition and inner wisdom. Finally, the crown chakra represents our connection to the divine.

As Kundalini moves upward, it cleanses and awakens each of these centers, leading to a profound transformation in both mind and body. What we experience along the way can be mystical, exhilarating, and at times, overwhelming. There may be moments of bliss, moments of intense purification, and moments of deep silence.

Symbols of Kundalini Energy

Kundalini is often symbolized by the serpent because of its coiled form. The serpent represents both the latent potential and the transformative power of the energy. In many cultures, the serpent is a symbol of wisdom, renewal, and rebirth. It sheds its skin, just as we must shed old identities, beliefs, and patterns during the process of awakening.

The upward movement of the serpent symbolizes the ascent of consciousness — from the base of the spine, where we are grounded in the material world, to the crown of the head, where we experience divine union and the realization of our true nature. This movement represents the journey of the soul toward enlightenment, breaking free from the limitations of the ego and merging with the infinite.

Another powerful symbol associated with Kundalini is the lotus flower. The lotus grows in the mud, yet its petals rise above the water, untouched by the dirt. This symbolizes the soul's journey — moving through the challenges and darkness of life, yet always rising toward the light. As Kundalini rises through the chakras, the lotus blooms, representing the unfolding of consciousness and spiritual awakening.

The Inner Experience of Kundalini

When the Kundalini energy awakens, the experiences can vary greatly from person to person. It is not a one-size-fits-all journey. Some may experience physical sensations — warmth or coolness along the spine, tingling in the limbs, or a sensation of energy flowing through the body. Others may experience more subtle shifts — an opening of the heart, an expanded sense of awareness, or a deep sense of peace.

But there are also challenges that come with awakening. Kundalini energy does not only bring joy and light; it also reveals the shadow. It stirs up unresolved emotions, fears, and past traumas that need to be healed in order for the energy to flow freely. This is why it is often said that awakening this energy requires preparation — not just physical, but mental and emotional. The mind must be strong, the heart must be open, and the body must be ready.

The experience of Kundalini can sometimes feel overwhelming, as the energy rises and purges old patterns. It is a purification process, which can be both exhilarating and frightening. It may involve intense emotional releases, flashes of insight, or a deep sense of surrender. It is important to approach the awakening process with patience, trust, and the understanding that it is not something that can be forced or controlled. It is a natural unfolding, a divine timing.

Kundalini and the Guru

In many traditions, it is said that the awakening of Kundalini should be guided by a teacher or guru. The guru is the one who has already awakened this energy and can guide the student safely through the process. This is why it is often said that Kundalini awakening should not be rushed or pursued recklessly. The energy is powerful, and when awakened prematurely or without proper guidance, it can cause imbalances or difficulties.

A true guru provides not just knowledge, but a living presence that can support the seeker's journey. Through their teachings and their example, they help the student navigate the challenges and breakthroughs that arise along the path. They create a safe container for the energy to rise, helping the student stay grounded and balanced.

The ultimate purpose of the Kundalini awakening is not just to experience a rush of energy or blissful states. It is to bring us back to the truth of who we are — to awaken us to our divine nature, to our connection with the source of all creation. As the energy rises, we shed the layers of the ego and the mind, and what remains is pure awareness — consciousness itself.

When the Kundalini reaches the crown chakra and merges with the infinite, the individual self merges with the universal self. The experience of separation dissolves, and we realize that we have always been one with the Divine. This is the state of samadhi — the highest state of consciousness, where the individual ego is dissolved, and only the pure essence of being remains.

Kundalini is not just a force of energy; it is the essence of life itself. It is the same energy that creates and sustains the universe. It is the life force that flows through every living being. Awakening this energy is the process of realizing our connection to all that is, and returning to the source from which we came.

As I look back on my own journey with Kundalini, I see it not as a distant, magical force, but as something deeply intrinsic to who I am. It is the energy of life — the pulse of the universe, the breath of creation. It is within us all, waiting to be awakened.

The question is not whether we will awaken this energy, but when we will be ready to embrace it. And when that moment comes, we will realize that it was never about the awakening itself, but about the return to the truth of who we always were.

CHAPTER 33
THE INNER GODS - AS ARCHETYPES OF CONSCIOUSNESS

For years, I had viewed the gods as figures in stories, detached from my daily life, subjects for religious devotion or mythological exploration. I'd heard their names — Shiva, Vishnu, Brahma, Ganesha, Devi, Murugan, and Hanuman — countless times, but their deeper meaning was elusive. It was only when I began to approach these divine archetypes through the lens of yogic wisdom that their true significance started to unfold, not as distant deities, but as powerful symbols of the inner landscape of consciousness.

In the yogic tradition, the gods are not separate from us; they are aspects of our own nature, embodied expressions of universal energies. They are not external beings to be worshipped from a distance, but reflections of the divine consciousness that resides within each of us. Each god represents a different facet of the mind, a different energy that shapes our thoughts, actions, and experiences. The gods are not outside — they are within.

Shiva — The Lord of Transformation

Shiva, the great destroyer, is perhaps the most misunderstood of the gods. To the uninitiated, destruction may seem negative or destructive, but in yogic terms, Shiva represents the transformative power of letting go. He is the force that dismantles old structures, outdated beliefs, and false identities, so that something new can emerge.

Shiva's dance — the Nataraja — is a symbol of the cyclical nature of creation, preservation, and destruction. In the yogic worldview, nothing is permanent. Life is a constant flow of creation and dissolution. The ego, the false sense of self that keeps us bound in illusion, must be destroyed for true liberation to occur. Shiva, as the destroyer, clears the path for new growth, new wisdom, and new beginnings.

When we connect with the energy of Shiva, we are invited to embrace the process of inner transformation — to burn away the old, to dissolve our attachments, and to move into a state of deeper awareness. Shiva teaches us that the death of the ego is not a loss, but a necessary step in the journey toward self-realization. His energy is the reminder that we must constantly let go of what no longer serves us in order to make space for the new.

Vishnu — The Preserver of Order

Vishnu, the preserver of the universe, represents the force that maintains cosmic harmony. While Shiva is the energy of destruction, Vishnu embodies the energy of preservation — the force that ensures that the universe operates in balance and order. Vishnu is the protector of Dharma, the cosmic law that governs the universe, and he is often depicted as taking incarnations (avatars) to restore balance when the world falls into chaos.

Vishnu's energy is the stabilizing force that holds the world together. In our own lives, Vishnu represents the principles of balance and harmony. He invites us to live in alignment with the natural flow of life, to honor the laws of nature, and to maintain inner peace amidst the chaos of the world.

When we invoke Vishnu, we tap into the energy of preservation. We are reminded of the importance of maintaining a sense of order within our lives — cultivating steady practices, honoring our duties, and living in alignment with the greater cosmic purpose. Vishnu teaches us that to preserve peace, we must first cultivate inner peace. His energy is the reminder that true balance comes from within.

Brahma — The Creator of the Universe

Brahma, the creator, embodies the creative force that brings forth the universe. He represents the energy of new beginnings, the spark of creation that animates all things. In yogic terms, Brahma is the source of all manifestation, the creative principle that gives birth to the material world.

Yet, Brahma's role is not just about external creation, but about the internal creative process. In our lives, Brahma represents the potential for creation — the spark of inspiration, the seed of new ideas, and the energy that motivates us to bring forth our dreams. To connect with Brahma is to connect with the energy of creation within ourselves — the creative spark that can manifest our highest visions.

Brahma teaches us that we are all creators, capable of shaping our own reality through our thoughts, actions, and intentions. By cultivating a deep awareness of the creative potential within us, we become co-creators with the universe, bringing new life and new possibilities into existence.

Devi — The Divine Mother

Devi, the goddess, represents the feminine principle of creation, nurturing, and transformation. She is the embodiment of Shakti, the dynamic energy that powers the universe. Devi is often depicted in various forms — Durga, Kali, Parvati, Lakshmi — each representing a different aspect of the feminine divine. But in all her forms, Devi symbolizes the creative, nurturing, and protective energy of the cosmos.

In yogic terms, Devi represents the force of Shakti — the primordial energy that flows through everything. She is the energy of creation, love, and abundance. Devi is the nurturing mother who nourishes all beings, guiding them toward their highest potential. She is the power that sustains life and the transformative force that can destroy ignorance and illusion.

When we connect with Devi's energy, we awaken to the nurturing, creative, and transformative force within ourselves. She invites us to embrace the power of love, compassion, and grace, to honor the feminine within and without, and to trust in the creative process of life. Devi teaches us that we must be both the nurturer and the nurtured, balancing strength with compassion, action with receptivity.

Ganesha — The Remover of Obstacles

Ganesha, the elephant-headed god, is revered as the remover of obstacles and the god of beginnings. He represents the energy that clears the path for new ventures, new opportunities, and new growth. But Ganesha is not only the remover of external obstacles; he is also the remover of internal barriers — the mental and emotional blockages that keep us from realizing our true potential.

In yogic terms, Ganesha's energy represents the power of clarity and understanding. He invites us to recognize and remove the obstacles within ourselves — the fears, doubts, and limiting beliefs that hold us back from living our fullest life. When we connect with Ganesha, we open ourselves to new possibilities and release the blockages that prevent us from moving forward on our path.

Ganesha teaches us that the first step to spiritual progress is the removal of internal and external obstacles. He is the reminder that, through awareness and action, we can clear the path toward spiritual growth and realization.

Murugan — The Warrior of Light

Murugan, the warrior god, represents the energy of courage, strength, and inner light. Known as the god of knowledge, wisdom, and spiritual battles, Murugan is often depicted with a spear, symbolizing his power to pierce through ignorance and illusion. He is the embodiment of inner strength, the ability to stand firm in the face of challenges, and the capacity to rise above worldly distractions.

Murugan's energy is one of spiritual fortitude — the courage to confront our own darkness and ignorance, and the wisdom to navigate the path of truth. When we connect with Murugan, we are reminded to be warriors on our own spiritual journey, to rise above fear and doubt, and to walk the path of righteousness with strength and clarity.

Murugan teaches us that the spiritual path requires both strength and wisdom. To overcome our own limitations, we must have the courage to face the challenges of life head-on, and the wisdom to understand that every obstacle is an opportunity for growth.

Hanuman — The Devotee and Symbol of Selfless Service

Hanuman, the monkey god, is the embodiment of devotion, humility, and selfless service. He represents the energy of surrender and love, and is revered as the greatest devotee of Lord Rama. Hanuman's strength lies not in his physical power, but in his unwavering devotion and selfless service to others.

In yogic terms, Hanuman's energy represents the path of bhakti, the path of devotion and surrender to the divine. He teaches us that true power lies not in force, but in love, humility, and service to others. Hanuman's unwavering devotion to Lord Rama serves as a reminder that surrendering to a higher purpose is not a weakness, but a source of inner strength.

Hanuman invites us to cultivate devotion, to live our lives with love, and to serve others selflessly. He reminds us that through devotion, we can transcend the ego and awaken to the divine presence within.

In understanding these gods as archetypes of consciousness, we realize that they are not separate entities, but reflections of the energies within us. They represent different aspects of our own inner nature, and by connecting with these energies, we learn to navigate the complexities of our inner world.

The divine is not outside of us; it is within us, waiting to be recognized, cultivated, and expressed. When we embrace these inner gods, we step into the fullness of our own being, living in alignment with the cosmic forces that guide and shape our existence. Through them, we begin to see that the path to awakening is not a journey to an external destination, but a return to the divine within.

PART VI
AWAKENING & INTEGRATION

CHAPTER 34
THE SEEKER BECOMES THE SEEN -
WHAT IT MEANS TO TRULY AWAKEN

There was a time when I believed that the journey of awakening was one of finding something — a truth, a state, a realization — that lay hidden just beyond my grasp. I searched through books, teachers, practices, and teachings, thinking that one day I would discover the elusive key to inner peace, to a higher state of being. I imagined myself as the seeker, tirelessly reaching for something outside of myself.

But the deeper I ventured into the practice of yoga, the more I realized that the true awakening is not about seeking something external at all. It is not about finding something outside of us. It is about remembering something that has always been within, something that was never lost. The true awakening is the moment when the seeker becomes the seen — when we recognize that the very search itself was part of the illusion.

The Illusion of Separation — The Seeker and the Sought

As we walk through life, we are conditioned to perceive ourselves as separate — separate from others, separate from nature, separate from the divine. The ego, with its thoughts and desires, constructs a sense of "I" and "other," creating a distance between us and everything else. We look outward, believing that our happiness, fulfillment, and purpose lie somewhere beyond us. The seeker is born from this illusion of separation.

But what happens when we peel away the layers of illusion, the beliefs, the ideas, and the stories we've been told? What remains when the distinction between the seeker and the sought disappears?

In yogic wisdom, the ego is seen as the great illusion — maya. It tells us that we are separate from the universe, that there is a "me" that is distinct from "you," from the world, from the divine. This illusion is so powerful that we forget our true nature, which is one with the infinite. The seeker, in this case, is a creation of the mind, a construct of the ego.

But when we begin to awaken, we start to see beyond the veil of separation. We start to realize that the seeker and the sought are not two different things — they are one and the same. The divine we seek is not outside of us, but within. The truth we are looking for is not distant or separate, but is the very essence of who we are. This is the moment when the seeker becomes the seen — when the illusion of separation dissolves, and we recognize the unity of all that is.

The Role of the Mind — The Witness and the Witnessed

In the process of awakening, the mind plays a pivotal role. The mind, which constantly seeks and desires, creates the illusion of separation. It is the mind that identifies with the ego, that believes in the story of "me" and "mine." But the mind also has the potential to become the witness — the observer of thoughts, emotions, and experiences. And it is in this role of the witness that true awakening begins.

When we stop identifying with our thoughts and emotions, when we learn to observe them without attachment or judgment, we begin to shift our perspective. We no longer see ourselves as the doer, the thinker, the feeler. We become the witness — the observer of all that arises and fades away. This shift in awareness is profound.

The witness does not cling to the past or the future; it exists in the present moment. It is a silent observer, detached from the story of the ego, yet deeply connected to the flow of life. The more we identify with the witness, the more we realize that the true self is not the thinker of thoughts, but the awareness that observes them. The awareness that is always present, even when the mind is restless or the emotions turbulent.

This realization is the key to awakening. It is the recognition that we are not the mind, the body, or the ego, but the awareness that witnesses all these things. The seeker, in this case, is the mind seeking to find something — but the true self is the awareness that has always been there, watching, witnessing, and simply being.

The Shift in Perspective — Becoming the Seen

True awakening is not a dramatic event. It is a subtle shift in perspective. It is the moment when we stop searching for something outside of ourselves and begin to realize that we are already the very thing we seek. The seeker becomes the seen — the search dissolves, and we rest in the awareness of what has always been present.

In that moment, we stop striving. We stop chasing. We stop trying to change who we are. Instead, we begin to embrace who we have always been. We begin to recognize that we are the Self — not a small, limited "me," but the vast, boundless consciousness that pervades all of existence. We are the divine, the infinite, the eternal.

This is the awakening — the realization that we are not separate from the universe, but one with it. That we are not the doer, but the witness. That we are not the seeker, but the seen.

Surrender — Letting Go of the Search

In the moment of awakening, there is a deep surrender. We surrender the search, we surrender the need to "find" or "achieve" anything. The paradox is that in letting go of the search, we find everything. In surrendering, we discover that what we were seeking was never lost. It was always within us, waiting to be realized.

This surrender is not a giving up; it is a letting go of the false sense of control that the ego clings to. It is a surrender to the flow of life, to the present moment, and to the divine presence that is within and around us. It is the recognition that we are part of a much greater whole, and that our true nature is not something we need to attain, but something we must simply remember.

The Return to the Self

The seeker becomes the seen in the same way that the wave returns to the ocean. The wave may rise and fall, but its true nature is always the ocean. Similarly, we may experience the fluctuations of the mind and the world, but our true nature is always the infinite consciousness — the Self. The seeker, in truth, is not separate from the sought. The seeker is the Self, seeking itself.

As I reflect on this journey, I realize that awakening is not about becoming something else. It is about remembering what we have always been. It is about returning to the source, the Self, the infinite presence that resides within us. The seeker becomes the seen when we recognize that there is no separation, no distance, no "other" to find. There is only the Self, already present, already whole, already awake.

In the end, awakening is not a destination. It is a realization. It is the realization that we have always been what we sought, and that the true nature of reality is not something to be attained, but something to be recognized. The seeker becomes the seen when the illusion of separation dissolves, and we rest in the truth of who we truly are — infinite, eternal, and awake.

CHAPTER 35
THE ROLE OF THE GURU - WHY A MASTER IS NEEDED, SURRENDER & TRANSMISSION

The concept of a guru had always seemed foreign to me, something distant, almost otherworldly. In my scientific worldview, the idea of surrendering to another person for wisdom felt contrary to my sense of individualism and independence. I had always believed that answers could be found through inquiry, through rational thought, through research and personal effort. The notion of submitting myself to a teacher — a master — seemed unnecessary, even outdated. But life, as it always does, had its own plan for me.

It was during one of my most confusing and challenging times, when my mind had reached the limits of its reasoning, that the need for a guru began to unfold in my life. I had spent years looking for answers in books, in theories, and in the external world. Yet, despite all the knowledge I had accumulated, something was still missing. I felt disconnected, like I was running on a treadmill — constantly moving but never getting closer to the destination I so deeply craved. It was clear that my mind alone couldn't bring me the inner peace and understanding I sought. The hunger for truth became louder, and no amount of intellectual exploration seemed to quench it.

That's when the concept of the guru started to resonate with me. The word "guru" comes from the Sanskrit root "gu," meaning darkness, and "ru," meaning light. The guru, in the truest sense, is one who dispels the darkness of ignorance and brings light to the soul. A true guru doesn't just teach; they illuminate the path, showing you the way to awaken your own inner wisdom. This was not a master who simply imparted knowledge, but a guide who helped you see beyond your own limitations — to awaken the dormant potential within.

But why did I, like so many others, need such a guide? The answer, as I soon discovered, was deeply personal.

A guru is not simply a teacher who provides answers. The guru is a doorway — a living bridge between the seeker and the higher truths. A true guru doesn't give you ready-made answers; they guide you back to your own truth, your own inner self. They help you remember what you already know but have forgotten. And this remembering — this awakening — happens not through intellectual understanding, but through experience. The transmission that occurs between the guru and the student is not merely of knowledge, but of energy, of vibration. It is a sacred transfer of consciousness that happens on a deeper, more subtle level.

In yogic tradition, this transmission is often referred to as shaktipat — the awakening of dormant spiritual energy within the disciple, facilitated by the guru. Through their presence, their words, their guidance, the guru activates the seeker's own potential, helping them connect with the divine within. It is not a process of learning from an external source, but of remembering one's true nature. The guru's role is not to dominate or control, but to act as a mirror, reflecting back the deepest truths of the self.

But this transmission can only happen through one thing: surrender.

Surrender does not mean giving up your will, nor does it mean submitting to blind authority. It is not about becoming passive or losing your individuality. Rather, surrender is about letting go of the ego's tight grip, allowing yourself to be open, vulnerable, and receptive. It's about acknowledging that there are things in life beyond the understanding of the mind — truths that cannot be grasped by intellect alone. To surrender to a guru is to acknowledge that there is wisdom beyond the individual self, that there is a higher guidance that transcends personal limitations. It is an act of trust, of opening oneself to the infinite flow of knowledge and energy.

In the presence of a true guru, the barriers of the mind begin to dissolve. The illusions of separation fade, and the realization that all is one begins to take root. Through this process of surrender, the seeker begins to transcend the limitations of their ego and opens up to the vastness of their own consciousness. This surrender is not about submission in the conventional sense, but about allowing oneself to be guided by the light of the guru's wisdom, and in turn, reconnecting with the light within oneself.

I experienced this truth personally when I met my own teacher. For the first time, I felt that I had been seen — truly seen — beyond the layers of my personality, beyond the masks I wore. In the silence of their presence, I felt a deep resonance, an energetic connection that went beyond words. It was in that moment I understood the true role of the guru: not as a person to be revered or worshipped, but as a reflection of the divine, a guide who leads you back to the divinity within yourself.

The teachings of the guru are not merely transmitted through words, but through the energy that flows between teacher and student. Every glance, every gesture, every moment shared is imbued with the sacred transmission of knowledge. In this way, the guru does not just teach you; they shape you. They challenge your illusions, break your attachments, and help you see beyond the confines of your individual self. Through this process, you are gradually drawn closer to your highest nature, the divine consciousness that exists within you.

In the end, the role of the guru is not to make you dependent on them, but to empower you to stand on your own, to walk your own path. The ultimate goal is for the disciple to become the teacher — to awaken to their own divinity and share that light with others. The true guru's wisdom lies in knowing that once the student has learned the lessons, they must be allowed to go, to walk their own journey. For the guru's ultimate purpose is not to be followed, but to help you realize that the wisdom you seek has always been within you.

And so, the circle completes itself. The guru appears, not as an external figure, but as a mirror reflecting your own divine nature. The transmission occurs, not through the exchange of information, but through the subtle energy of the soul. And the surrender is not the loss of self, but the discovery of the true self, which has always been there, waiting to be awakened.

The journey with the guru is not a destination; it is the beginning of the inner journey. Through their guidance, you realize that the master you sought outside was always waiting within.

CHAPTER 36
THE YOGIC WAY OF LIVING - BRING AWARENESS INTO DAILY LIFE

The ancient wisdom of yoga is not confined to the four walls of a meditation hall or the peaceful space of a yoga mat. It is a living practice, woven into the fabric of daily life. I once thought of yoga as something that happened on the mat, a place to stretch, breathe, and connect with myself. But the more I learned, the more I realized that yoga is not something we do — it is something we live. It is a way of being, a way of relating to the world, a way of connecting to the deeper truth within us.

Yoga, at its core, is about awareness. It is about waking up from the slumber of automatic, unconscious living and stepping into a more conscious, intentional way of being. It's about remembering who we truly are and bringing that remembrance into every moment, every action, and every interaction.

The First Step — Awareness

The first step in living a yogic life is simply awareness. It seems so simple, but in reality, it is the most profound shift we can make. Most of us go through life on autopilot — reacting to the world around us without thinking, without fully experiencing, without being present. We rush from task to task, distracted by the noise of the mind and the busyness of the world. But in the practice of yoga, we learn to slow down and to be present.

Awareness begins with noticing the body — how it feels, what it needs, how it moves. But it doesn't stop there. Awareness extends to the mind — noticing the thoughts that arise, the emotions that pass through, the stories we tell ourselves. And it extends to our relationships — how we communicate, how we listen, how we connect. Awareness is about being fully present in each moment, without judgment, without distraction, and with complete acceptance.

When we bring awareness into our daily life, everything changes. We stop being carried away by the current of the world and begin to choose how we respond, how we act, and how we relate. Yoga teaches us that the power of transformation lies not in grand gestures or distant retreats, but in the simple, everyday moments of our lives.

The Yoga of Everyday Actions

Every action we take, every word we speak, every thought we think is an opportunity to practice yoga. Yoga is not just the physical postures; it is also the way we walk, the way we eat, the way we interact with others. In fact, the true test of yoga is not how we perform a pose, but how we live in the world.

The yogic way of living teaches us to bring awareness to every moment, even in the simplest tasks. Washing dishes becomes an act of mindfulness. Cooking becomes a prayer. Walking becomes a meditation. Listening becomes an offering. The way we treat others — with kindness, patience, and respect — becomes an extension of our practice.

The yogic texts speak of karma yoga, the yoga of selfless action, which encourages us to act in the world without attachment to the results. When we bring this principle into daily life, we stop doing things for the approval or recognition of others. We act because it is the right thing to do, because it is aligned with our deeper values and truth. We offer our actions as a gift to the universe, and in doing so, we find joy and peace in the process, not just in the outcome.

Breath and Presence — The Foundation of Yogic Living

The breath is the foundation of yoga. It is the bridge between the body, mind, and spirit. Through conscious breathing, we can access a deeper state of presence and awareness, and bring ourselves back to the present moment, no matter what is happening around us. The simple practice of mindful breathing — inhaling fully, exhaling completely — can transform any moment into a sacred one.

In daily life, we can bring the breath into everything we do. When we feel stressed, overwhelmed, or disconnected, we can pause, take a deep breath, and return to the present moment. This simple practice grounds us and reawakens our connection to ourselves. It allows us to step out of the mental noise and into the space of peace and stillness.

The breath also teaches us the importance of balance. In yoga, we learn to balance effort and ease, tension and relaxation, activity and stillness. This balance can be applied to every aspect of life. We learn to approach our tasks with focus and commitment, but also with a sense of ease and flow. We learn to work hard, but not at the expense of our well-being. We learn to rest and recharge, knowing that both effort and relaxation are necessary for a fulfilling life.

The Practice of Compassion — Ahimsa in Daily Life

One of the most fundamental principles of yoga is ahimsa — non-violence. This is not just about avoiding physical harm; it is about practicing kindness, compassion, and understanding in every aspect of life. Ahimsa begins with how we treat ourselves — with love, care, and acceptance. It extends to how we treat others — with respect, empathy, and forgiveness. And it extends to how we treat the planet — with reverence, gratitude, and stewardship.

Living with compassion means being mindful of the energy we put into the world. It means speaking with kindness, acting with consideration, and thinking with love. It means letting go of judgment and embracing understanding. It means recognizing the divine in every person we meet, every animal, every plant, and every being. It means seeing the interconnectedness of all life and acting from a place of love and unity.

Surrender to the Flow — Trusting the Universe

Another key aspect of living the yogic way is surrender. Surrender does not mean giving up or resigning ourselves to fate. It means trusting the flow of life, trusting that everything is unfolding as it should, even when we don't understand it. It means letting go of control and allowing the universe to guide us, knowing that we are always supported.

In everyday life, this surrender looks like letting go of expectations, attachments, and the need to control outcomes. It is about trusting that life will unfold in its own time and that we are exactly where we need to be. It is about practicing patience and faith, knowing that every experience, whether joyful or painful, is part of our growth and transformation.

Integration — Yoga Beyond the Mat

The yogic way of living is about integrating the practice into every aspect of life. It is not something we do for an hour a day and then forget about. It is something we live. It is about bringing awareness, kindness, balance, and surrender into every moment. It is about living with intention, not just in our yoga practice, but in everything we do — from the way we wake up in the morning, to the way we interact with others, to the way we take care of ourselves and the world around us.

Yoga is a holistic path that encompasses the body, mind, and spirit. It teaches us to live with awareness, compassion, and purpose, to recognize the divine in every moment, and to trust the unfolding of life. It is not just a set of practices; it is a way of being in the world — a way of living with consciousness, love, and presence. And when we live this way, we align with the deepest truths of who we are and experience the joy and freedom that come from living in harmony with the universe.

In the end, yoga is not just something we practice; it is the way we live. It is the way we show up in the world — with awareness, love, and presence. It is the path of becoming who we truly are, in every moment, in every breath. And as we walk this path, we discover that the true practice of yoga is not about achieving anything at all — it is about remembering everything that we already are.

CHAPTER 37
THE UNVEILING OF THE DIVINE TRUTH

Understanding the Purpose of Life Through Yogic Science and Living a Life of Awareness, Love, and Liberation

Every journey begins with a question—a spark of curiosity that leads us down paths we never imagined we'd travel. My journey began with an innocent yet profound inquiry: What is life? Why are we alive? What started as an intellectual, almost scientific, quest, soon unraveled into something far more intimate, far more profound. What I once thought was a problem to be solved—like an equation waiting to be cracked—slowly revealed itself as something much deeper. Life, I discovered, is not something to be measured or quantified. It is not a puzzle to be solved, nor a mystery to be decoded by mere intellect. It is something to be felt, something to be experienced, something to be remembered—not through the senses or the intellect, but through the essence of being itself. Not outside, but within.

Through the lens of yogic science, I didn't gain a new belief system. I wasn't given a set of answers or prescribed dogmas. What I received were tools—tools that opened a doorway not to another world, but to this very one. A world that was always here, waiting for me to see it clearly for the first time. It was not about transcendence, but about presence. It was about peeling away the layers of illusion, so that I could experience the purity of the present moment, unencumbered by preconceived notions or mental constructs.

Yogic science taught me that life is not random. It is not a chaotic accident, nor is it a cold, mechanistic process. Life is rhythmic. It is intelligent. It is sacred. Every breath, every thought, every emotion, every experience is intricately woven into the grand fabric of existence. We are not isolated beings, but part of a vast, interconnected web that pulses with energy, purpose, and meaning. At the very core of this web, at the center of it all, lies awareness—the witness, the observer, the silent presence that sees, without judgment or attachment, the unfolding of creation. Awareness is the essence of who we are, and it is the key to understanding life's true purpose.

But this path, this profound awakening, is not meant to be walked alone.

In the vast and sometimes overwhelming inner terrain of consciousness, there is a need for guidance—a presence that illuminates the way forward. This presence is not an external force, nor is it someone who simply hands us answers. Rather, it is a Guru, a true guide who helps us peel away everything that is false, everything that distracts us from our deepest truth. The Guru does not give us truth; they help us uncover it from within. They do not add more layers to our understanding—they help us remove the ones that veil our innate wisdom. The Guru does not control us; they awaken us to our own divinity, our own potential. Without such a guide, the seeker may wander endlessly in the labyrinth of their own mind, unsure of the next step, lost in confusion.

A true Guru is not someone to be worshipped from a distance. The Guru is a mirror, reflecting back to us the truth that already resides within. The Guru's grace is subtle, quiet, but its effects are life-changing. In their presence, transformation becomes not a difficult struggle but a natural unfolding. The seeds of awakening that lie dormant within us all are stirred by their presence, and with time, they begin to sprout and bloom.

To walk the path of yoga is to walk with humility, devotion, and openness. It is to surrender to the process, to let go of the ego's need for control and perfection, and to embrace the journey with trust and faith. In the presence of such a guide, the path becomes not only clearer but also more joyful and effortless. The challenges we face are no longer burdens but opportunities for growth, and the journey itself becomes a dance of awareness and love.

The true revolution is not to be found in the outer world, in grand ideas or political movements. The real revolution is the transformation of consciousness. It is the ability to live each moment with awareness, to be rooted in love—not attachment, but love in its purest, most selfless form. It is the capacity to walk this Earth with stillness in the mind and compassion in the heart. This, I realized, is the essence of liberation. True freedom comes not from escaping the world, but from embracing it fully, with clear eyes and an open heart.

The purpose of life is not some distant, elusive truth hidden in the stars. It is here, in this moment, in this breath, in this body, in this experience. And when we live through awareness, life transforms into something sacred. Life becomes a temple—a space where the Divine is not worshipped from afar but remembered within. Each breath, each heartbeat, each moment becomes a prayer, a living offering to the sacredness of existence.

I used to search for truth only outside—believing it was locked away in formulas, in particles, in theories that could be proven or disproven. I sought the answers in books, in science, in the observable world. But now, yoga has invited me to look within. Not to abandon logic or reason, but to deepen it, to understand it from the inside out. Yoga has taught me that truth is not something to be discovered externally, but something to be realized through practice—through direct experience.

This, I have come to understand, is my new beginning. A new way of being, a new way of seeing, a new way of living. A path that honors awareness, personal experience, and inner transformation. This is not a path of dogma or blind faith; it is a path of direct experience, of living the truth through every breath, every action, every thought.

And so, with an open heart and a clear mind, I step onto the yogic path. The journey of self-realization, the journey to reconnect with the Divine, the journey to uncover the infinite wisdom that resides within.

CHAPTER 38
THE SECRET OF LIFE

As I reach the final pages of this journey, it becomes clear that it was never about finding an answer that could be neatly written down, explained, or packaged in a way that could be easily taught to another. It was never about reaching some final destination. The truth, if it can be called such, was always about the experience itself.

From the moment we are born, the human mind is on a quest — a quest for meaning, for purpose. We ask ourselves, "Why am I alive? What is the meaning of all this? What am I truly meant to do?" In our search for answers, we instinctively turn outward. We chase after love, success, security, companionship. We seek comfort in possessions, validation in relationships, and fulfillment in achievements.

We pursue everything outside of ourselves, thinking that what we seek is somewhere out there—hidden in the world, in the approval of others, in the next moment or the next experience. Yet, no matter how much we gather, something remains unfinished, unresolved, incomplete. The joy we find outside of ourselves is often fleeting. Love, when contingent on the approval or presence of another, turns into longing. Peace, when anchored in changing circumstances, is perpetually disturbed. The mind creates expectations, and the world, as it often does, fails to meet them.

And from that gap between expectation and reality, suffering arises. But it is important to understand: the suffering is not created by life itself. Life is not inherently painful. The pain arises from the stories we tell ourselves, from the meaning we impose on our experiences. The thoughts, the judgments, the perceptions — these are the source of our agony, not life as it truly is.

We carry pain, not because life is inherently cruel or unjust, but because we resist what is. We get entangled in desires that are not even ours, living lives dictated by external influences, by societal pressures, by the stories others have written for us. We live out scripts that reflect everything except our own true, authentic nature. And in this unconscious living, we forget who we are — not in a philosophical sense, but in the deepest, most existential way.

But the moment we shift our gaze inward — when we turn away from the external world and the never-ending pursuit of "more" — something begins to shift. In the quietude of this inward turn, something stirs. Not the silence of a quiet room, not the absence of sound, but the silence that exists beyond thought, beyond identity, beneath the layers of the ego, deep within the pulse of breath. This is the silence of the present moment, the space where the noise of the world falls away, and only awareness remains.

As awareness deepens, the seeker who once sought answers starts to fade. The one who once believed life had to be figured out, who desperately tried to solve the riddle of existence, begins to realize: I am life itself. There is no "me" separate from the very thing I sought. In this moment of recognition, the boundaries of identity dissolve.

The peace that was once sought in external conditions, in circumstances beyond our control, is suddenly discovered at the very source—within. The love once craved from others now rises naturally from within one's own being. The joy that was always momentary, always elusive, when found outside, becomes a continuous, unshakable presence within. Inwardly, the human being does not transform into something new; rather, they remember what they have always been — whole, complete, and unified with the very essence of existence.

And in that remembrance, something extraordinary unfolds. The boundaries that once seemed so real — the distinctions between "me" and "you", "self" and "other" — begin to fade into irrelevance. The individual self, which once clung so tightly to its separate identity, begins to merge with the presence of the moment. The drop of water, once so focused on its own individuality, merges into the ocean and realizes that it was always the ocean pretending to be a drop. There is no longer any separation between the individual and the universe; both are one, inseparable.

Here, in this space, there are no grand proclamations, no final and climactic revelations that can be captured in words. There is only the endless unfolding of truth. No dogma, no doctrines, no rigid belief systems — only truth as it is experienced, not conceptually, but directly.

This, then, is the secret of life.

It is not in becoming someone, but in simply being. It is not in acquiring knowledge of everything, but in the deeper, transformative knowledge of yourself. Not as a name, not as a body, not as a narrative or identity, but as pure awareness, as consciousness, as life itself — that which transcends all labels, all distinctions, all limitations.

This is the purpose of life: to remember what you are, to awaken to the truth that has always been present within you. This is the pathless path, the answer behind all questions. It is not something you find in the world outside; it is something you become in the quiet, intimate spaces of your own being.

In the end, it is not the answers that matter, but the experience itself. The experience of being present with life, of merging with its flow, of realizing that you are not separate from it but an integral part of it. This is the experience of life itself — the ultimate truth.

CHAPTER 39
LET THE JOURNEY BEGIN - A HEARTFELT BEGINNING TO DEEPER INNER PRACTICE, OPENNESS TO EXPERIENCE, SURRENDER

As I sit here, reflecting on all that has been explored, all the questions that have emerged and the answers that have slowly started to weave themselves into my awareness, I realize something deeply important:

This is only the beginning.

The journey that began with curiosity, with questions, with the thirst for truth, has brought me to a place where I can no longer stay stagnant. The words have stirred something within me, a calling to deepen my practice, to live this truth, to embody it fully in every moment.

But what does it mean to begin this journey?

It's not about making grand declarations or finding some grand plan. It's about opening myself to the unfolding. It's about stepping into the unknown with nothing but trust in the process, with no expectations except to be present to what comes.

To truly begin is to surrender — to let go of all that I think I know, to release the illusion of control, and to open myself to whatever arises. Every moment, every experience, every encounter is part of this sacred journey, and each one is a reflection of the greater whole.

This journey is not one of force, but of receptivity. Not one of struggle, but of surrender.

I remember the first time I heard the word surrender. It felt like a loss, like giving up. I thought, "If I surrender, does that mean I stop fighting? Stop seeking?" But surrender is not about giving up. It's about giving in — giving in to the flow of life, to the dance of existence. It's about trust — trust that everything is unfolding as it should, and that I am not separate from it.

The practice of surrender is the practice of letting go of all my attachments to the outcome. It is the willingness to be with what is, without resistance. To sit with the discomfort of not knowing, and the vulnerability of not having all the answers.

Surrender isn't about weakness; it's about strength. Strength to remain open. Strength to remain present. Strength to say, "I don't need to control this. I am a part of something much bigger."

And so, the practice begins — not as something to be done, but as something to be lived. It's about bringing awareness to every moment — from the simple acts of breathing, walking, and eating, to the complex emotions and thoughts that arise within me. Every moment is an invitation to practice — to be fully awake, fully present.

I'm beginning to understand that every step I take on this path is a step inward, a step toward remembering the truth of who I am. The external journey is, in many ways, a reflection of the inner one. The more I surrender to this process, the more I realize that there is no destination — only the unfolding. I do not need to become anything. I simply need to be.

The path of surrender is the path of opening — opening to the infinite possibility of life, to the unknown that calls me forward. It is not about control. It is about letting life move through me, guiding me in ways I cannot yet understand.

As I begin this deeper practice, I open myself fully to the experience. I release the need to label, to judge, to force anything. Instead, I simply surrender to the journey. Every experience becomes a gift. Every moment a lesson. Every step a prayer.

So here I stand, at the edge of this vast and endless journey. With nothing but trust, I take the first step, knowing that this path will continue to unfold in ways that may be unexpected, but all of which will bring me closer to the truth I've been seeking. I am ready.

Let the journey begin.

FINAL REFLECTION - THE JOURNEY WITHIN

As this book comes to a close, I invite you to pause — not just to reflect on the words you've read, but to feel into the silent space between them.

This has never been just a book of ideas, teachings, or traditions. It has been a journey — one that mirrors the eternal path of the seeker. A journey that begins not in the stars or scriptures, but in a quiet inner longing. A whisper that says: There must be more than this.

We've explored science and its questions, yoga and its revelations, mythology and its meanings. But the essence of the journey has never been about answers — it has always been about deepening the question. About awakening the part of you that watches, listens, and gently asks: Who am I, really?

Every concept, every chakra, every story and teaching was not meant to be the destination, but a door. A door back to yourself.

The ancient sages knew this. They knew that all seeking ultimately leads to the same place — the center of your own being. The Self, timeless and luminous, waiting patiently beneath the layers of thought, habit, and illusion.

If something stirred within you as you turned these pages — a feeling of resonance, recognition, or even restlessness — let it be your guide. The journey doesn't end here. It never does. In fact, this may only be the beginning.

Close this book not as a conclusion, but as a continuation. Let what you've read become what you live. Let it inform how you breathe, how you act, how you see the world — and more importantly, how you see yourself.

You are the seeker.

You are the seen.

You are the journey.

And you have always been home.

A NOTE TO THE READER

If you've arrived here — to the last page — then you've not only walked through this book, but through a sacred part of your own unfolding.

Thank you for staying with me, for breathing through the questions, and for allowing your heart to open in the spaces between the words. It means more than you know.

You have not just read these pages — you have remembered something timeless within yourself. Something that doesn't belong to any tradition, lineage, or teacher. It belongs to you. It always has.

This was never just my journey. It was always yours, too.

The truths we explored, the stories we unfolded, the energies we spoke of — they are now seeds planted in your own inner soil. You don't need to carry everything forward. Just carry what resonates. Let it breathe inside you. Let it grow in its own rhythm.

Above all, walk your path — your way — with courage, curiosity, and love. Let the mystery remain alive. Let wonder guide you. Let the silence between the answers be your true teacher.

Because the seeker is not someone who follows. The seeker is someone who remembers. And in that remembrance, they begin to truly see.

From the stillness of my heart to the unfolding of yours — thank you. This is not the end. This is the beginning of your own becoming.

With reverence and love,
From one seeker to another

ACKNOWLEDGEMENTS & GRATITUDE

Before this book could ever take shape in words, it lived as a quiet flame — a yearning, a remembrance, a call from within. To that silent guide — the inner voice, the eternal witness — I offer my deepest gratitude.

To the unseen teachers, whose presence may never be known by name or form but whose wisdom whispers through intuition, stillness, and synchronicity — I thank you. You have led without leading, and taught without speaking.

To the great river of Yogic knowledge, carried through the hearts of sages, rishis, and Siddhars across millennia — I bow. This work stands not on my own insight, but on the shoulders of those who preserved this light through silence, sacrifice, and surrender.

To the living traditions of Yoga and Sanatana Dharma — not merely as systems of thought, but as living, breathing streams of realization — thank you for allowing me to taste even a drop of your infinite depth.

To the land of Bharat — sacred mother, soil of saints and seekers — may your wisdom forever guide the world back to truth.

To those in my life who held space for this journey — through your patience, love, and presence — I am humbled and grateful.

And to you, dear reader — fellow seeker — thank you for walking this path. Your openness, your courage to question, and your willingness to go inward are the very spirit of this book. Whether we ever meet in this lifetime or not, know that your presence here matters.

This offering is for you.
May it serve your path.
May it remind you of who you already are.

With reverence,
— Deepak Sekar

ABOUT THE AUTHOR

Deepak Sekar is not a guru, nor a scholar — he is simply a seeker. A soul drawn by questions too vast for answers, by a silence too deep for words.

His journey began with science — stars, atoms, and equations. But when life broke open, so did the questions. The laws of physics could explain the how, but never the why. And so, the search turned inward.

From ancient yogic wisdom to the silent teachings of the Siddhars, from sacred sound to the stillness of being — Deepak Sekar followed the thread of truth wherever it led. Not to escape life, but to understand it. To live it more fully. To remember what it means to be.

The Seeker's Journey: From Science To Self is his first offering — a deeply personal and poetic reflection of the inner path. It is not written to teach, but to hold space. A companion for fellow seekers walking their own way home.

This Page Is For Your Remembrance

Close your eyes.

Be still.

Let the Lamp within you speak.